Workshop on Technologies for MT of Low Resource Languages (LoResMT 2018)

Held at AMTA 2018

Boston, Massachusetts, USA
21 March 2018

ISBN: 978-1-5108-6730-7

Printed from e-media with permission by:

Curran Associates, Inc.
57 Morehouse Lane
Red Hook, NY 12571

Some format issues inherent in the e-media version may also appear in this print version.

Printed by Curran Associates, Inc. (2018)

Association for Computational Linguistics
209 N. Eighth Street
Stroudsburg, Pennsylvania 18360

Phone: 1-570-476-8006
Fax: 1-570-476-0860

acl@aclweb.org

Additional copies of this publication are available from:

Curran Associates, Inc.
57 Morehouse Lane
Red Hook, NY 12571 USA
Phone: 845-758-0400
Fax: 845-758-2633
Email: curran@proceedings.com
Web: www.proceedings.com

Contents

AMTA 2018
March 17 - 21, 2018
Boston, MA, USA

The 13th Conference of
The Association for Machine Translation
in the Americas
www.conference.amtaweb.org

WORKSHOP PROCEEDINGS
March 21, 2018

Technologies for MT of Low Resource Languages (LoResMT 2018)

Organizer: Chao-Hong Liu *(ADAPT Centre, Dublin City University)*

Introduction
AMTA 2018 Workshop on Technologies for MT of Low Resource Languages (LoResMT 2018)

Recently we have observed the developments of cross-lingual NLP tools, e.g. MLP 2017 Shared Tasks on Cross-lingual Word Segmentation and Morpheme Segmentation and IJCNLP 2017 Shared Task on Customer Feedback Analysis. The results showed clearly now we are able to build one NLP system for multiple languages in a specific task and the system can perform very well compared to its monolingual counterparts. The development of this kind of cross-lingual tools will be very beneficial to the many low resource languages and will definitely improve machine translation (MT) performance for these languages. We would like to see if this idea could be further extended and realized in other NLP tools, e.g. several kinds of word tokenizers/de-tokenizers, morphology analyzers, and what impacts these tools could bring to MT systems.

In this workshop, we solicit work on the NLP tools as well as research on MT systems/methods for low resource languages in general. The scopes of the workshop are not limited to these tools for MT pre-processing and post-processing. We would like to bring together researchers who work on these topics and help review/overview what are the most important tasks we need from these tools for MT in the following years.

Two speeches on organized events dedicated to this line of research in China and Russia will be given. Our speakers will also give the overview of NLP tools developed for and research on minority languages in China and Russia. Seven papers are archived in the proceedings, in which languages involved include Catalan, Finnish, Filipino, Irish, Korean, Latvian, Quechua, Russian, Sámi, Tibetan, Turkic languages, as well as Mandarin Chinese, French and English.

I would like to express my sincere gratitude to the many researchers who helped as advisers, organizers, and reviewers and made the workshop successful. They are Alberto Poncelas, Alex Huynh, Alina Karakanta, Daria Dzendzik, Erlyn Manguilimotan, Francis Tyers, Hamidreza Ghader, Iacer Calixto, Ian Soboroff, Jonathan Washington, Josef van Genabith, Koel Dutta Chowdhury, Majid Latifi, Marzieh Fadaee, Nathaniel Oco, Peyman Passban, Prachya Boonkwan, Qun Liu, Sangjie Duanzhu, Santanu Pal, Sivaji Bandyopadhyay, Sudip Kumar Naskar, Thepchai Supnithi, Tommi Pirinen, Valentin Malykh, Vinit Ravishankar, Wei Bao, Yalemisew Abgaz, as well as colleagues in ADAPT Centre. I am thankful to AMTA organizers Steve Richardson, Priscilla Rasmussen and Olga Beregovaya for their continuous help on the workshop from the very beginning. We are very grateful to the authors who submitted their work to the workshop. Xiaobing Zhao, Bei Wang, Valentin Malykh and Varvara Logacheva, who prepared the two invited speeches are much appreciated. Thank you so much!

Boston, March 2018

Chao-Hong Liu
Workshop Chair
ADAPT Centre
Dublin City University
Glasnevin Dublin 9, Ireland.

Acknowledgements

The ADAPT Centre for Digital Content Technology is funded under the SFI Research Centres Programme (Grant No. 13/RC/2106) and is co-funded under the European Regional Development Fund. The organization of this workshop has partially received funding from the European Union's Horizon 2020 Research and Innovation programme under the Marie Skłodowska-Curie Actions (Grant No. 734211).

Organizing Committee

Organizers

Alina Karakanta	Universität des Saarlandes
Chao-Hong Liu	ADAPT Centre, Dublin City University
Daria Dzendzik	ADAPT Centre, Dublin City University
Erlyn Manguilimotan	Weathernews Inc., Japan, formerly with NAIST
Francis Tyers	Higher School of Economics, National Research University
Iacer Calixto	ADAPT Centre, Dublin City University
Ian Soboroff	National Institute of Standards and Technology (NIST)
Jonathan Washington	Swarthmore College
Majid Latifi	Universitat Politècnica de Catalunya - BarcelonaTech
Nathaniel Oco	National University (Philippines)
Peyman Passban	ADAPT Centre, Dublin City University
Prachya Boonkwan	National Electronics and Computer Technology Center
Sangjie Duanzhu	Qinghai Normal University
Santanu Pal	Universität des Saarlandes
Sivaji Bandyopadhyay	Jadavpur University
Sudip Kumar Naskar	Jadavpur University
Thepchai Supnithi	National Electronics and Computer Technology Center
Tommi A Pirinen	Universität Hamburg
Valentin Malykh	Moscow Institute of Physics and Technology
Vinit Ravishankar	Charles University in Prague
Yalemisew Abgaz	ADAPT Centre, Dublin City University

Program Committee

Reviewers

Alberto Poncelas	ADAPT Centre, Dublin City University
Alex Huynh	CLC Center, University of Science, VNU-HCMC-VN
Alina Karakanta	Universität des Saarlandes
Chao-Hong Liu	ADAPT Centre, Dublin City University
Daria Dzendzik	ADAPT Centre, Dublin City University
Erlyn Manguilimotan	Weathernews Inc., Japan, formerly with NAIST
Francis Tyers	Higher School of Economics, National Research University
Hamidreza Ghader	University of Amsterdam
Iacer Calixto	ADAPT Centre, Dublin City University
Jonathan Washington	Swarthmore College
Koel Dutta Chowdhury	ADAPT Centre, Dublin City University
Majid Latifi	Universitat Politècnica de Catalunya - BarcelonaTech
Marzieh Fadaee	University of Amsterdam
Nathaniel Oco	National University (Philippines)
Peyman Passban	ADAPT Centre, Dublin City University
Santanu Pal	Universität des Saarlandes
Sivaji Bandyopadhyay	Jadavpur University
Sudip Kumar Naskar	Jadavpur University
Thepchai Supnithi	National Electronics and Computer Technology Center
Tommi A Pirinen	Universität Hamburg
Valentin Malykh	Moscow Institute of Physics and Technology
Vinit Ravishankar	Charles University in Prague
Yalemisew Abgaz	ADAPT Centre, Dublin City University

LoResMT 2018 Program

Session 1

09:00AM–10:30AM

Introduction to LoResMT 2018 Workshop — Chao-Hong Liu

INVITED TALK
Research and Development of Information Processing Technologies for Chinese Minority/Cross-border Languages — Bei Wang & Xiaobing Zhao

Using Morphemes from Agglutinative Languages like Quechua and Finnish to Aid in Low-Resource Translation — John E. Ortega & Krishnan Pillaipakkamnatt

Break **10:30AM–11:00AM**

Session 2

11:00AM–12:30AM

SMT versus NMT: Preliminary comparisons for Irish
Meghan Dowling, Teresa Lynn, Alberto Poncelas & Andy Way

Tibetan-Chinese Neural Machine Translation based on Syllable Segmentation
Wen Lai, Xiaobing Zhao & Wei Bao

A Survey of Machine Translation Work in the Philippines: From 1998 to 2018
Nathaniel Oco & Rachel Edita Roxas

Lunch **12:30PM–02:00PM**

Session 3 **DeepHack.Babel**

02:00PM–03:30PM

INVITED TALK
DeepHack.Babel: Translating Data You Cannot See
Valentin Malykh & Varvara Logacheva

Semi-Supervised Neural Machine Translation with Language Models
Ivan Skorokhodov, Anton Rykachevskiy, Dmitry Emelyanenko, Sergey Slotin & Anton Ponkratov

System Description of Supervised and Unsupervised Neural Machine Translation Approaches from “NL Processing” Team at DeepHack.Babel Task — Ilya Gusev & Artem Oboturov

Break — **03:30PM–04:00PM**

Session 4 — **Tools, Demos, Discussions**

04:00PM–05:30PM

Apertium’s Web Toolchain for Low-Resource Language Technology
Sushain Cherivirala, Shardul Chiplunkar, Jonathan North Washington & Kevin Brubeck Unhammer

Demos and Discussions

Closing.

Invited Talk
Research and Development of Information Processing Technologies for Chinese Minority/Cross-border Languages

Bei Wang bjwangbei@qq.com
National Language Resource Monitoring and Research Center,
Minority Languages Branch, Minzu University of China

Xiaobing Zhao nmzxb_cn@163.com
National Language Resource Monitoring and Research Center,
Minority Languages Branch, Minzu University of China

Natural Language Processing for Chinese minority languages is a challenging and important task. In this talk, we will present the current status of Chinese minority languages, including the situations in general of 56 ethnic groups in China and 33 different groups of cross-border languages used by 30 cross-border ethnic population in China. Secondly, research on minority languages information processing and its difficulties and challenges will be presented. We will also introduce notable projects and scientific publications on minority languages information processing. Specifically, we will give an overview of the minority language word segmentation task we held in 2017, as well as the work we have done on Chinese minority languages natural language processing in our center.

Biography

Prof. Xiaobing Zhao is the chair of National Language Resource Monitoring & Research Center, Minority Languages Branch, Minzu University of China. Xiaobing Zhao obtained her M.S. degree in Artificial Intelligence from Chungwoon University in 2003, and her Ph.D. in Computational Linguistics in Beijing Language & Culture University in 2007. Xiaobing Zhao has published more than 50 papers, authored 2 books and 1 China National invention patent. She has supervised 13 PhD students and 10 master students. Xiaobing Zhao has undertaken a number of small or large scale projects, including Chinese NSFC Key projects, "863" Key projects, provincial and ministerial Key projects, among others. Xiaobing Zhao has won the first prize of Qian Weichang Science and Technology Award, second prize of Science & technology Development/Achievement of the Ministry of Education the ministry of education, first prize in scientific and technological achievements of the State Archives Administration of the People's Republic of China, and other awards.

Invited Talk
DeepHack.Babel: Translating Data You Cannot See

Valentin Malykh valentin.malykh@phystech.edu
Moscow Institute of Physics and Technology

Varvara Logacheva logacheva.vk@mipt.ru
Moscow Institute of Physics and Technology

Neural networks were introduced in Machine Translation (MT) quite recently and immediately became state of the art in the field. Today their advantage over phrase-based statistical MT systems is unquestionable and neural networks are used in the majority of online MT engines. What is more important, neural MT beats SMT not only in usual data-rich scenario, but also allows accomplishing tasks which are impossible for SMT systems.

One of the recent notable advances in the field of MT is training of a translation model without parallel data. This task could not be fulfilled by SMT systems which need sentence-aligned datasets to extract the translation variants. One approach is to use a model called auto-encoder to train neural Language Models (LMs) for source and target languages. Such LMs create a representation of a text in a multi-dimensional space. These spaces can be merged so that both source and target sentences can be represented in the same space. With such a pair of LMs a source text can be converted to a vector in this space and then to a textual representation in the target language — which gives us an MT system trained on two unrelated monolingual corpora.

Our hackathon was inspired by these works. In order to make the task easier we relaxed the task. Instead of unsupervised MT we formulated the task of the hackathon as semi-supervised MT — MT which is trained on a very small parallel dataset and larger monolingual corpora for both source and target languages. This scenario is also more realistic. While pairs of languages with no parallel data are quite rare, there exist many pairs where parallel texts exist, but are scarce. In such cases it is desirable to improve MT systems with monolingual corpora.

The hackathon lasted for five days, which of course did not allow to train a state-of-the-art MT model. However, our corpora were relatively small (50,000 parallel sentences and 0.5–1 million monolingual sentences). We also imposed restrictions on the size of models and on training time, so that participants have time to train their models, get results and make changes several times within these five days. In order to spare participants from re-implementing existing models we allowed use of open-source implementations of MT systems. On the other hand, the task was complicated by domain discrepancy between the parallel and monolingual data.

One of the features of our hackathon was hidden training data. We had three sets of corpora, each consisting of a small parallel training corpus, a pair of relatively fair in size monolingual corpora and small parallel dataset for testing. One of these sets was given to participants to make them familiar with the format and let them tune their models. That was Ru-En set, since most of the participants are proficient in both languages. Another set for a different language pair was used for the evaluation of models during hackathon. Neither the dataset itself nor the language pair were not disclosed to participants. They submitted their models, they were trained and tested in a blind mode. The third (hidden) dataset was used to produce the final scores and define the winner in the same manner. The first and the third sets share a feature of domain skew between parallel corpus and monolingual corpora, while the second does not.

The main aim of hiding the data was to prevent participants from cheating — e.g. collecting extra data for a language pair instead of training on the provided datasets. In addition to that, it served for making the scenario more language-independent. The majority of algorithms used for the MT task are in principle language-independent in the sense that they use the same principles for most of languages. Despite that, many common techniques are more effective on languages with poor morphology and "standard" (Subject-Verb-Object) predominant word order. The success of MT systems for other languages often depends not on algorithms, but on additional tweaks which deal with word order errors and rich morphology. By ruling out the information about properties of source and target languages we check the efficiency of MT algorithms themselves and have a possibility to see to what extent they can handle the challenges of a particular language pair.

The majority of participants used the following scenario. They used parallel corpora to train an initial translation model which was initialised with word embeddings trained on monolingual corpora. After that they translated monolingual datasets with this model and retrained it using this synthetic parallel data. Nevertheless, some teams used unsupervised models as a part of ensemble models.

Biographies

Valentin Malykh is a researcher and a PhD student at Moscow Institute of Physics and Technology. His research interests are dialogue systems, in particular robustness to noise in input and style transfer in dialogues. Valentin has been co-organising DeepHack events since 2016, and he also co-organised ConvAI — a competition of chatbots which took part at NIPS-2017.

Varvara Logacheva is a researcher in Moscow Institute of Physics and Technology. She got a PhD in Computer Science from the University of Sheffield, where she was a member of Natural Language Processing group. The main topic of her thesis was Quality Estimation for Machine Translation and its integration into MT systems. Her present research interests are dialogue systems, in particular non-goal-oriented dialogue systems (chatbots) and their automatic and manual evaluation. Varvara has been co-organising track on Quality Estimation for MT at WMT since 2015. She also co-organised ConvAI in 2017.

Using Morphemes from Agglutinative Languages like Quechua and Finnish to Aid in Low-Resource Translation

John E. Ortega jeo10@alu.ua.es
Dept. de Llenguatges i Sistemes Informatics, Universitat d'Alacant, E-03071, Alacant, Spain

Krishnan Pillaipakkamnatt csckzp@hofstra.edu
Department of Computer Science, Hofstra University, Hempstead, NY 11549, USA

Abstract

Quechua is a low-resource language spoken by nearly 9 million persons in South America (Hintz and Hintz, 2017). Yet, in recent times there are few published accounts of successful adaptations of machine translation systems for low-resource languages like Quechua. In some cases, machine translations from Quechua to Spanish are inadequate due to error in alignment. We attempt to improve previous alignment techniques by aligning two languages that are similar due to agglutination: Quechua and Finnish. Our novel technique allows us to add rules that improve alignment for the prediction algorithm used in common machine translation systems.

1 Introduction

The NP-complete problem of translating natural languages as they are spoken by humans to machine readable text is a complex problem; yet, is partially solvable due to the accuracy of machine language translations when compared to human translations (Kleinberg and Tardos, 2005). Statistical machine translation (SMT) systems such as Moses [1], require that an algorithm be combined with enough parallel corpora, text from distinct languages that can be compared sentence by sentence, to build phrase translation tables from language models. For many European languages, the translation task of bringing words together in a sequential sentence-by-sentence format for modeling, known as word alignment, is not hard due to the abundance of parallel corpora in large data sets such as Europarl [2]. In contrast, Quechua is a language that is spoken by more than nine million people in South America (Adelaar, 2012); yet, parallel texts with Quechua in them are very scarce (Monson et al., 2006).

This paper presents an approach to address the scarcity problem of parallel corpora in Quechua. In particular, we compare our approach with a previous approach that attempted to align Quechua to German (DE) using DE as the pivot language with the final translation being Spanish (Rios et al., 2012). Generally, the consensus on solving language translation with little resources is to find more resources or use rule-based, instead of statistical-based, machine translation through employing a more controlled corpus, or set of texts like the ones presented in the Avenue project [3].

[1] `http://www.statmt.org/moses/`
[2] `http://www.statmt.org/europarl/`
[3] `https://www.cs.cmu.edu/~avenue/`

Additionally, scarce-resource languages like Quechua seldom have translated technical corpora like Europarl available. We attempt to employ Natural Language Processing (NLP) techniques to better align Quechua words to other, more widely studied, words in Finnish. Specifically, techniques such as pronoun identification (Lee et al., 2013), are considered by this paper to be the key strategies in attempting to find a solution to the scarcity problem.

Moses [4] builds translation tables from models and texts that are aligned from word alignment tools like Giza++ [5], the alignment module that Moses uses to pre-align text before applying heuristics to find the most likely translations from a bank of possibilities (Och and Ney, 2003). Giza++ is used to align words from sentences in parallel text. For example, the following sentence in English: "I_1 $love_2$ you_3" would directly align with its parallel German counterpart: "Ich_1 $liebe_2$ $dich_3$" by applying a one-to-one alignment where a position x in the English sentence is directly aligned to a position y in the German sentence.

The overall probability scheme used in Giza++ for the first major iteration is called the Expectation-Maximization (EM) probability (Do and Batzoglou, 2008). The focus in this paper is to review and adapt the tools that are most widely used for SMT (namely Moses and Giza++) to prove that linguistic rules that label pronouns and their counterparts can be added to obtain more accurate results for specific languages such as Quechua, a highly agglutinative language (Rios, 2011).

In the case of Quechua, most parallel texts use Spanish as the target language. Constitutional documents, plays, and poetry can be found in parallel format from various sources (Llitjós, 2007). Unfortunately, Spanish is not easily aligned to Quechua due to the complex Quechua morphology that uses suffix-based grammatical determination in order to modify words that are morphological and syntactically different from those of Spanish.

Our hypothesis is that it may be easier to take two "naturally" similar languages and compare their grammatical similarities in order to better align the languages. Most previous research attempts to translate Quechua to some other common target language, such as Spanish, have been unsuccessful due to the complexity of alignment. We leverage the abundance of Quechua–Spanish (QU–ES) corpora with the abundance of (ES–FI) text to create a final Quechua–Finnish (QU–FI) system to compare against previous work. Our aim is to modify EM algorithmic heuristics in Giza++ to achieve better Alignment Error Rates (AER) than previously published by empowering the alignment that Quechua and Finnish possess.

Moses generally uses BLEU scores to measure the preciseness of a translation. Previous work does not seem to have published Quechua translation BLEU scores because BLEU scores are normally used when there is an abundance of corpora available for the languages at hand. Our system is a hybrid rule-based and phrase-based (statistical) machine translation (MT) system for translating from Quechua to Finnish where Spanish is used as a pivot (helper) language and Giza++ is used for aligning Quechua words to Finnish words.

2 Related Work

Various researchers have attempted tasks like detecting entities such as nouns, verbs, and pronouns in Quechua. Several of the more important projects are based on research efforts completed in a project called the Avenue project (Llitjós, 2007). The Avenue project was created to serve as a parallel corpus project that implemented NLP tools such as a spell checker. Spell checkers, unfortunately, are not translation tools and do not attempt to map one language to another through translations. Nonetheless, spelling correctors and other editing tools can be useful for reviewing Quechua corpora's correctness of word spelling in order to ensure more precise input to a more sophisticated word alignment or machine translation tool.

[4] http://www.statmt.org/moses/

[5] http://www.statmt.org/moses/giza/GIZA++.html

Research has been completed by Rios et al. (2012) at the University of Zurich that uses the Avenue Elicitation Corpus (Llitjós, 2007). Particularly, they have performed a substantial amount of research on aligning Quechua to Spanish and vice-versa. The University of Zurich tree-banks are an attempt to annotate Quechua with the correct Part-of-Speech (POS) tags. They have taken an inflective approach by identifying suffix inflections and assigning each inflection as part of a numerical inflection group. Their work has established a good baseline research point for Quechua experimentation and is helpful with the task of translating Quechua to Spanish. However, most research completed to this date, including the Rios et al. (2012)'s research, seems to deal with the Quechua language as a whole and its translation to Spanish rather than focusing on the specific language construction and morphology. Here, we use linguistic rules to show that morphemes from Quechua to Finnish align better due to the linguistic similarity of the two languages.

Another series of morphology experiments, similar to those done at the University of Zurich, were performed by Nießen and Ney (2004). Their methodology reduced the original corpus size about ten percent resulting in only a 1.6 percent loss of translation quality while using inflectional grouping. The idea implemented by Nießen and Ney (2004) is similar to the idea researched by Rios et al. (2012) that we use for comparison in this paper. By classifying morphemes into specific inflections, or lack of inflections, groups can be formed to better statistically decide where a source word may align to a target word. The inflection idea was originally proposed by researchers at IBM (Ecker et al., 1999). Quechua is in its majority is based on inflectionally-grouped suffix morphemes. We use that phenomenon to develop a hybrid machine translation system based on Moses and Giza++. The main focus of our work is to show that rules can be applied to Quechua that will improve the error rates from Giza++ alignment results in the work performed by the University of Zurich - Parallel tree-banking Spanish-Quechua(Rios et al., 2012).

3 Language Specifics

Quechua is morphologically rich. Its morphology is comparable to many other European languages such as Finnish, Turkish, and even French. Quechua is a language that heavily depends on word parts, knows as morphemes, being added on as suffixes; hence, we say that Quechua is agglutinative (Rios, 2011). One example of its agglutinativity is seen with the infinitive verb in Quechua for the English verb "to grow", "wiña". The suffix "nku" is added to the word "wiña" to form the Quechua third-person plural verb, "wiña-nku", which translates to the English words "they grow". The English translation does not change the infinitive form of the word. Rather, in English, it is grammatically correct in many cases to simply add the word "they" in front of the infinitive verb to create the third-person plural form of the infinitive. It is noted that Quechua contains as many as 130 these types of suffixes (Göhring, 2014) - we deal with two of them in our work.

4 Methodology

We attempt to improve the Alignment Error Rates (AER) achieved by University of Zurich (Rios et al., 2012) by duplicating the results (QU–DE and QU-ES) using the same corpora and resources from their project. Then, we modify the final growth-and-reordering algorithm that Moses provides from the Giza++ alignment. It is important to note that our focus will be on the alignment ideas performed by Rios et al. (2012); therefore, we use IBM Model 1 and its lexical matching as a first step rather than focus on other, more complicated, models. All of the corpora used in this project coincide with the corpora used in the tree-banking project at the University of Zurich (Llitjós, 2007).

After duplicating the AER published by Rios et al. (2012), we create reference sentences in Finnish. This is done by translating the previous (Spanish) reference sentences to Finnish using a Moses system trained on Europarl. Then, we manually align Quechua words to Finnish words. Slight adaptations were made to the original target reference sentences. However, the difference can be considered negligible (less than 2 words on average per sentence).

With the reference corpora created, we modify Giza++'s algorithm for alignment, the EM algorithm presented in the book by Koehn (2009), by adding practical pronoun possessive rules. After rule insertion, we rerun a new Moses (QU–FI) execution and record alignment rates by comparing the new output to our reference corpora.

4.1 Alignment Technique

The alignment technique we use attempts to naturally align Quechua with another language that has more readily available corpora - Finnish. Finnish has been chosen because it is quite agglutinative and, in many cases, suffix-based grammatical rules are used to modify words in the Finnish language similar to Quechua. In order to better exemplify agglutination, the example below is presented:

- Infinitive Finnish verb "to correct": korja
- Conjugate Finnish verb "to correct": korjaame (stem is korjaa)
- Infinitive Quechua verb "to correct": allinchay
- Conjugate Quechua verb "to correct": allinchaychik (stem is allinchay)

There are two main figures from the word evaluation summary table published in the parallel tree-banking paper (Rios et al., 2012) that are of most concern: 1) Spanish to Quechua words and 2) Spanish to Quechua inflectional groups. Respectively, the Alignment Error Rate (AER) achieved by the Zurich group are: 1) 85.74 and 2) 74.05. The approach taken in the parallel tree-banking paper is to use inflectional groups that will group word parts, known as lexicons (Becker, 1975), in order to translate unknown source (Spanish) words. Since Giza++ attempts reverse translations, it could be determined that a reverse translation from Quechua to Spanish would also produce around eighty percent AER. That is because the parameters used in Rios et al. (2012)'s work do not align null words and use the default methods for alignment in Giza++. The rules are not necessarily supervised because they use inflection groups(IG). An IG is a way of applying a tag to a word by annotating it according to a classification with a specific group as was done by Rios et al. (2012).

Quechua is based on a morphological structure that depends on suffixes to determine the meaning of root words that would otherwise be infinitive verbs. We modify the EM algorithm from Koehn (2009) to increase the likelihood of a word containing a desired morpheme match that has not been classified. That way matches are always done on words found in the past rather than a group of phrases. We modify the EM algorithm because other models, outside of IBM Model 1 and IBM Model2, are commonly based on fertility (Schwenk, 2007) and, thus, are not helpful when attempting to translate scarce-resource languages like Quechua. Furthermore, applying probabilities to words that cannot be aligned by a phrasal approach, where the "null" qualifier is allowed, could actually harm the output. For our purpose, which is to produce better alignment error rates than those presented in the University of Zurich parallel tree-banking project (Rios et al., 2012), all models with exception of IBM Model 1, are excluded leaving a single sentence iteration for probability purposes. While a single iteration may not be the most optimum execution operation for likelihood expectation, it serves well as a determinant for the rule-based probability. One can imagine aspects of the higher order IBM models that don't involve fertility could be useful. e.g., aspects involving distance or relative distance between matching words.

We also show that using Spanish as the pivot language for translations to Finnish makes suffixes, or morphemes, easier to align and makes inflectional grouping less necessary. Rules can be added that simply start at the end of the source word and compare them to the end of the target word. Each suffix has its own meaning and use that can be aligned using rule-based heuristics to determine the best word match. Our experiments described below show that the result of changing the target language increases the probability of lower alignment error rates.

Finnish has been chosen here for detecting pronouns through suffix identification. Pronouns in Finnish are in many cases added to the end of the stem word, or lemma, in order to signify possession or direction much like is done in Quechua. While we were unable to identify all of the suffixes with their pronouns in Quechua, we show that by adding two pronoun and possession rules we achieve higher AER.

Finnish is also ideal because rendering of Finnish sentences from Spanish sentences using a version of Moses trained on Europarl is easier than Quechua to Spanish. That makes choosing a pivot language, such as Spanish, the ideal candidate for translating the QU–ES texts to QU–FI texts and vice-versa. And, while the use of Finnish alone may be considered one of the most important factors in the alignment experiment, the focus of this paper is the adding of rules to the suffixes of both languages in order to better the AER found in previous QU–ES experiments.

Here we are working with lexical alignment between two like languages, one with low resources available. That makes a pivot language necessary. The advantage of translating by using a pivot language without a bilingual corpus available has been shown in the past by Wu and Wang (2007). By using the pivot language, we are able to translate Quechua to Finnish without having any Finnish translations directly available for Quechua. We use Finnish as the target language and Spanish as the pivot language for the alignment strategy of logical word pairing between Finnish and Quechua through their similar suffix incorporation.

5 Experiments

5.1 Tools, Corpora, and Algorithm

In order to have a clear image of how the results are achieved, we define the tools, corpora, and other necessaries of the research performed. The main tool used for attaining research results, Moses, is a combination of various tools and corpora. Apart from Moses, other auxiliary tools such as Aulex [6], an on-line translator, have been used to modify the corpora and their corresponding configuration files. Altogether, an extended amount of time was spent on preparing the input and reference sentences used for improving the alignment error rates. We use Moses for translation experiments.

There are three major phases that take place when translating a document in Moses: 1) Tokenization and Parsing, 2) Word Alignment, and 3) Phrasal and Word Tuning. For this project, the translation from Quechua to Finnish relies heavily on the first two phases above: Tokenization and Word Alignment.

Our final language model has a vocabulary from the words found in the corpora, both native and foreign, Quechua and Finnish, respectively. After preparing a model with probabilities for each word, word alignment is performed with the Giza++. We add suffix pronoun rules in order to gain higher percentages on words that are easily aligned from Quechua to Finnish.

Lastly, after word alignment is completed and saved, Moses performs final tuning and smoothing that uses statistics to determine phrase probability in the phrasal step. In our case, we only perform one alignment step of a lexicon type that compares suffixes word by word and applied commonality, or expectation, through learned words from the corpora.

As seen in Table 1, the three steps required to successfully modify rules to process

[6] `http://aulex.org`

Quechua to Finnish translations using Giza++ and Moses can be complex.

Step 1: Tokenize and Parse	**Step 2:** Word Alignment	**Step 3:** Phrasal Tuning
1. create the initial corpora 2. prepare corpora for word alignment 3. translate from Spanish to Finnish	1. apply suffix rules 2. parallel word alignment from Quechua to Finnish	1. extract word phrases 2. build translation table 3. word reordering 4. tuning

Table 1: Steps for translating Quechua to Finnish in Moses using our proposed hybrid MT system

Altogether, our corpus contains 450 sentences. The SQUOIA corpora [7] from the University of Zurich tree-banking project, in its original textual format, are quite diverse and require various manual efforts in order to get quality parallel sentence translations. In order to get both the Finnish and Quechua texts in a readable format, manual reading and some command line tools are used. On-line dictionaries and publications from the following list are used create and align the parallel corpora:

- http://tatoeba.org
- http://www.runasimi.de
- http://aulex.org
- http://www.folkloredelnorte.com.ar

Apart from dictionaries, consultations from native speakers on a non-organizational basis were requested in order to review the reference sentences. But, reference sentences are not necessarily as important due to the fact that statistics, apart from the repeated occurrences of a particular word or lexicon, are not heavily used. The native speakers simply confirm that reference sentences are grammatically and logically correct.

Tools like Tixz [8] and Picaro [9] are used for alignment visualization in order to clearly view the aligned words and predict the AER (Alignment Error Rate) for the translated sentence results. In order to get results, the alignment configuration and results files have to be extracted from Moses because they are part of the overall system processing.

In order to nearly duplicate results from the University of Zurich, we execute Moses on the corpora from SQUOIA project [10] with the same parameters defined: 1) Null values are not allowed as a word 2) Fertility is not used and 3) Lexical matching is used. As an overall parameterized machine, the idea is to do word-forward matching based on the training corpora model that Giza++ creates during a single iteration. This is done by modifying the configuration file in Moses for IBM Model 1 only and adding rules directly into the IBM Model 1 EM algorithm. The basic idea of IBM Model 1 is that by applying the Chain Rule (Ambrosio and Dal Maso, 1990) of probability with two steps:

[7] `https://code.google.com/archive/p/hltdi-l3/wikis/PossiblyUsefulCorpora.wiki`
[8] `http://texample.net/`
[9] `http://www.isi.edu/~riesa/software/picaro/`
[10] `http://a-rios.github.io/squoia/`

1. Expectation application of the model and

2. Maximization estimation of the model

from the data, conversion should occur that will align native (e) words with foreign (f) words.

Since we use 446 sentences for training, probability from word references in sentence pairs alone is not enough to predict the final phrasal probability. Generally speaking, the main problem with scarce resources and statistical probability on lexical matching is the global count, or maximization of probability. The Maximization step from the EM algorithm for SMT in Moses written by Koehn (2009) takes the counts of probability and applies them at the end of execution. But, if there are few sentences in the corpus, probability cannot be skewed highly for a particular word because the amount of text that coexists in a phrasal situation is relatively low. Word alignment cannot be high (greater than fifty percent) if the sentences available are scarce. In order to maximize probability on our desired suffix rules, we modify the Em Algorithm for IBM Model 1 right before collecting counts [11].

5.2 Rule Addition

Modifying the Giza++ alignment algorithm for Finnish and Quechua requires a detailed understanding of Quechua and Finnish morphology. We use a few of the grammatical suffix rules from both languages that have the same meaning and convert them into rules that can be applied to the EM algorithm. Two pronoun-based rules are presented to show that the possibility for alignment error exists:

1. "chik" in Quechua to "me" in Finnish

2. "yki" in Quechua to "si" in Finnish

In order to better understand the two rules presented here that are added to the Giza++ EM algorithm, a review of both grammars and the effect of their corresponding suffixes presented above is necessary.

Rule 1 presented above is the "chik" suffix in Quechua. CHIK is a word that is a pronoun type by nature because it describes a particular part of speech: third person inclusive "we". This behavior can be seen in word like "riku-wa-n-chik". The Quechua verb "rikuy" means "to see" in English. By adding the "wa", "n", and "chik", the verb is converted into a third person group that collectively means "we see". There are exceptions to the rule. CHIK appears as "nchik" following a vowel, "ninchik" following a consonant, and "chik" elsewhere (as when it follows the "n" morpheme) (Lewis et al., 2009). Clearly, a pronoun suffix rule can be added to the EM rule in order to achieve the "we" functionality desired by adding a coefficient to the probability of the word match $p(e, f|a)$ and $p(f, e|a)$. The additional thirty-three percent of probability is added to words that fully comply with Rule 1. The inclusive third person pronoun "we" in Quechua is equivalent to the suffix in Finnish "me". The possessive suffix "mme" is compulsory in standard Finnish [12]. Finnish words that end with "me" are, thus, words that can be aligned directly with Quechua words that end with "chik". It is important to note that there are exceptions. But, considering the high error rate that currently exists (more than fifty percent), it makes sense to add this type of rule. Apart from that, the idea of explicit pronoun resolution between Quechua and Finnish has not been performed previously to our knowledge. The University of Zurich project and other projects have centralized attention on specific parts of speech and inflectional groups without specifying the specific pronoun alignment. We attempt to show

[11] line 17 of the EM algorithm on page 91 (Koehn, 2009)

[12] using standard Finnish dictionary from `http://en.wiktionary.org/wiki/-mme`

that the location of words within sentences in Quechua makes pronoun resolution somewhat possible between Quechua and Finnish. And, based on the amount of text that is available in Finnish and Spanish, pronoun resolution and specific positioning within larger corpora could possibly be attained.

Rule 2 is similar to Rule 1 in that it is based on pronoun resolution. This rule is more interesting because it directs attention to the singular second person pronoun "you". On top of that, the suffix "yki" signified that the first person is directing the root word toward the second person like the word for "I love you" in Quechua "munakuyki". The "yki" suffix is used when subject "I" does something to the direct pronoun "you", also known as the "I you" suffix (Ruiz, 2006). A direct word for word alignment from Quechua to Spanish in the example above would be almost impossible due to the amount of words in a Spanish phrase for "I love you", "Te quiero", and a Quechua word like "Munakuyki", a two-to-one comparison. Since null values are not permitted in this experiment, "munakuyki" could only be aligned to one word. Finnish does not always directly align to Quechua. For example, the Finnish equivalent for "I love you", like Spanish, is also two words, "Rakastan sinua". Nonetheless, there are more suffix-based words in Finnish that align to Quechua pronoun suffixes than in English or Spanish. That makes translating Quechua to Finnish much easier. The Finnish equivalent for the Quechua word "yki" is "si". Therefore, as is done in Rule 1, the application of probability will applied in foreign and native sentence to reflect the rule by giving a higher percentage to those words that comply with the rule. We add a 33% coefficient to rules that meet the desired requirement by modifying counts in the EM algorithm in Koehn (2009):

$$\text{count}(e|f) = \frac{t(e|f)}{total_{s(e)}} + \mathbf{.33}$$

The change will ensure that the global probability calculated for all sentences produces a higher percentage for words that are an exact lexical match for the rules proposed in here.

6 Results

In general, previous AERs show that when translating Quechua to Spanish, Moses and Giza++ produce high error rates as Table 2 confirms:

Univ. of Zurich Results	F_s	F_p	AER
ES–QU words	11.64	15.20	85.74
Lowercase ES–QU words	12.62	15.57	85.02
ES–QU Inflectional Groups	25.40	25.84	74.05
Lowercase ES–QU Inflectional Groups	26.53	26.89	72.95

Table 2: Original ES–QU results from the University of Zurich (Rios et al., 2012) where F_s represents sure alignments, F_p represents possible alignments, and AER represents the alignment error rate.

A QU–FI execution is done with the our new, hybrid Moses system that contains two new suffix pronoun rules. As mentioned before, each counts probability has a possibility of changing by a coefficient of .33 when a rule has been met. For this experiment, there are about 12 words per sentence and one sentence per line. That means that around 6000 words have to be compared for alignment between Quechua and Finnish. Table 3 shows the hybrid rule addition results.

Our Hybrid Suffix-Based Results	F_s	F_p	AER
FI–QU words	12.21	15.08	85.62
Lowercase FI–QU words	14.07	14.61	85.02
FI–QU Inflectional Groups	34.13	34.17	64.71
Lowercase FI–QU Inflectional Groups	34.00	34.13	61.08

Table 3: Hybrid suffix-based FI–QU results where F_s represents sure alignments, F_p represents possible alignments, and AER represents the alignment error rate.

The results confirm that there are grammatical rules that can be applied directly to the suffix of a word from either language to improve alignment in the new system. That is not possible when comparing Spanish to Quechua. There are complexities when comparing the agglutinative language, Quechua, to the separated language, Spanish. There is clearly a difference between translating suffix-based translation groups in parallel word-for-word text from sentences and translating phrases that may occur in phrase-based translation with languages that are less agglutinative.

There are a large amount of suffixes that could fall under the two rules and it is clear that the AER presented may be decreased even further by classifying all of the possibilities as suffix type rules. It should be noted that, while the rules do somehow indicate supervised learning, the learning applied here is non-deterministic by nature due to the fact that grammatical construct is used as the basis for comparison for parallel words and sentences instead of a dictionary-based or single lexicon match. We leave other MT systems and forms of learning such as Zoph et al. (2016) out for this paper; but, it's would be worthwhile to try for future iterations of the system.

7 Conclusions

By adopting a "first-things-first" approach we overcome a number of challenges found in developing NLP Systems for resource scarce languages (Monson et al., 2006). After comparing the same reference sentences introduced in the initial experiment to our results, our work has shown successful results using suffix rules for pronouns.

The research performed has given a clear example of the possibilities of hybrid machine translation techniques with languages that have few resources available. Quechua is as an example of a low-resource spoken in various South American countries. The two rules here that are added into Giza++ are just two possibilities of the various combinations of suffixes that occur between Finnish and Quechua. Rules could be extended in Giza++ that would include all of the possibility suffixes in order to gain the best possible translation. Giza++ itself, as a word alignment tool, could be modified to accept hybrid-based rules in order to accept specific probabilities through a configuration file much like it currently does with dictionaries. The amount of possibilities that this project opens is endless. Giza++ modification is only one manner of extending this project to be applied to others.

References

Adelaar, W. F. (2012). Modeling convergence: Towards a reconstruction of the history of quechuan–aymaran interaction. *Lingua*, 122(5):461 – 469. Language Contact and Universal Grammar in the Andes.

Ambrosio, L. and Dal Maso, G. (1990). A general chain rule for distributional derivatives. *Proceedings of the American Mathematical Society*, 108(3):691–702.

Becker, J. D. (1975). The phrasal lexicon. In *Proceedings of the 1975 Workshop on Theoretical*

Issues in Natural Language Processing, TINLAP '75, pages 60–63, Stroudsburg, PA, USA. Association for Computational Linguistics.

Do, C. B. and Batzoglou, S. (2008). What is the expectation maximization algorithm? *Nature biotechnology*, 26(8):897.

Ecker, D. M., Duan, L., Franz, A. M., and Horiguchi, K. (1999). Analyzing inflectional morphology in a spoken language translation system. US Patent US6442524B1.

Göhring, A. (2014). Building a spanish-german dictionary for hybrid mt. In *Proceedings of the 3rd Workshop on Hybrid Approaches to Machine Translation (HyTra)*, pages 30–35.

Hintz, D. J. and Hintz, D. M. (2017). The evidential category of mutual knowledge in quechua. *Lingua*, 186:88–109.

Kleinberg, J. and Tardos, E. (2005). *Algorithm Design*. Addison-Wesley Longman Publishing Co., Inc., Boston, MA, USA.

Koehn, P. (2009). *Statistical machine translation*. Cambridge University Press.

Lee, H., Chang, A., Peirsman, Y., Chambers, N., Surdeanu, M., and Jurafsky, D. (2013). Deterministic coreference resolution based on entity-centric, precision-ranked rules. *Computational Linguistics*, 39(4):885–916.

Lewis, M. P., Simons, G. F., Fennig, C. D., et al. (2009). *Ethnologue: Languages of the world*, volume 16. SIL international Dallas, TX.

Llitjós, A. F. (2007). *Automatic improvement of machine translation systems*. Carnegie Mellon University.

Monson, C., Llitjós, A. F., Aranovich, R., Levin, L., Brown, R., Peterson, E., Carbonell, J., and Lavie, A. (2006). Building nlp systems for two resource-scarce indigenous languages: mapudungun and quechua. *Strategies for developing machine translation for minority languages*, page 15.

Nießen, S. and Ney, H. (2004). Statistical machine translation with scarce resources using morpho-syntactic information. *Computational linguistics*, 30(2):181–204.

Och, F. J. and Ney, H. (2003). A systematic comparison of various statistical alignment models. *Computational linguistics*, 29(1):19–51.

Rios, A. (2011). Spell checking an agglutinative language: Quechua. In *5th Language and Technology Conference: Human Language Technologies as a Challenge for Computer Science and Linguistics*, pages 51–55.

Rios, A., Volk, M., et al. (2012). Parallel treebanking spanish-quechua: how and how well do they align? *Linguistic Issues in Language Technology*, 7(1).

Ruiz, C. S. (2006). *Quechua, manual de enseñanza*, volume 4. Instituto de estudios peruanos.

Schwenk, H. (2007). Building a statistical machine translation system for french using the europarl corpus. In *Proceedings of the Second Workshop on Statistical Machine Translation*, pages 189–192. Association for Computational Linguistics.

Wu, H. and Wang, H. (2007). Pivot language approach for phrase-based statistical machine translation. *Machine Translation*, 21(3):165–181.

Zoph, B., Yuret, D., May, J., and Knight, K. (2016). Transfer learning for low-resource neural machine translation. *arXiv preprint arXiv:1604.02201*.

SMT versus NMT:
Preliminary comparisons for Irish

Meghan Dowling meghan.dowling@adaptcentre.ie
Teresa Lynn teresa.lynn@adaptcentre.ie
Alberto Poncelas alberto.poncelas@adaptcentre.ie
Andy Way andy.way@adaptcentre.ie
ADAPT Centre, Dublin City University, Glasnevin, Dublin 9, Ireland

Abstract

In this paper, we provide a preliminary comparison of statistical machine translation (SMT) and neural machine translation (NMT) for English→Irish in the fixed domain of public administration. We discuss the challenges for SMT and NMT of a less-resourced language such as Irish, and show that while an out-of-the-box NMT system may not fare quite as well as our tailor-made domain-specific SMT system, the future may still be promising for EN→GA NMT.

1 Introduction

In recent times, NMT has been widely hailed as a significant development in the improvement in quality of machine translation (MT). However, as a technique that is data-hungry, there is a concern that languages with fewer resources may not benefit to the same degree that well-resourced major languages do. In order to prevent a low-resource language such as Irish being left behind in the context of these advancements, we take the first steps towards applying NMT methods to English→Irish (EN→GA) translation.

Irish is the national and official language of the Republic of Ireland, and an official EU language. While EN→GA MT is rarely used for comprehension purposes,[1] MT is invaluable in meeting the language rights needs of native Irish speakers. MT has already been proven useful in the post-editing environment of an official Irish government department, where the translation of EN→GA documents has been facilitated by a Moses-based statistical machine translation (SMT) system (Dowling et al., 2015). The success of this domain-specific SMT system is due in part to the availability of high quality parallel data in this particular domain (see Table 1). The quality of MT is currently unreliable for official translation in an EU setting, however. This is partly due to a derogation imposed on the production of official Irish language texts in the EU.[2] While the European Commission is moving towards using NMT engines in the new eTranslation platform,[3] Irish is not yet sufficiently supported.

Despite a relatively low availability of resources – in terms of both bilingual and monolingual digital content – we have previously shown that a domain-tailored SMT system can achieve promising translation quality (Dowling et al., 2015).[4] The question remains whether NMT can

[1]Most (if not all) Irish speakers have fluency in English.

[2]`http://publications.europa.eu/code/en/en-370204.htm`

[3]`https://ec.europa.eu/cefdigital/wiki/display/CEFDIGITAL/Machine+Translation`

[4]Results: BLEU .43/ TER .46

achieve a similar level of usability for Irish in this setting. While the introduction of deep learning methods to the field of MT has witnessed a breakthrough in recent years, the positive impact of NMT is not felt across the board. As Koehn and Knowles (2017) highlight, current NMT systems can face a number of challenges when dealing with specific tasks. These challenges include low-resourced languages, low-frequency words arising from inflection, long sentences, and out-of-domain texts. The latter may not apply to our test case, as the success of our earlier SMT system lies in the closed domain nature of the use case (public administration data), yet the other factors are very real for the Irish language in general. In this study, we report on recent scores from the training of an updated Irish SMT engine, based on our latest data sets. We then present a preliminary NMT baseline, based on the same training and test data as previous SMT experiments, in order to investigate its strengths and weaknesses with respect to Irish.

The paper is divided as follows: Section 2 provides the context within which our work is relevant, both in terms of low-resourced MT and the use of MT in professional translation environments. In Section 3 we outline the datasets we use in training and testing, and give some background on the types and sources of this data. Section 4 details how the SMT and NMT experiments were implemented. Section 5 provides updated results for EN-GA SMT in this domain and establishes preliminary results for EN-GA NMT. Finally, in Section 6 we provide some conclusions and indicate possible options for future work in this area.

2 Related Work

As discussed above, currently the primary focus of the application of Irish MT is within the context of a professional translation workflow (involving post-editing by human translators), and as such, progress in this area in terms of advances in state-of-the-art approaches is of interest to us. For many years, there have been extensive studies to show how the integration of MT within such a workflow (often complementary to the use of translation memory tools) improves productivity, both in industry-based and in academic-based research (e.g. Etchegoyhen et al. (2014); Arenas (2008)). With the introduction of NMT methods, there have been subsequent studies examining the differences between the impact that SMT and NMT have within such a setting. For example, Bentivogli et al. (2016) carried out a small scale study on post-editing of English→German translated TED talks, and concluded that NMT had made significantly positive changes in the field. Bojar et al. (2016) report a significant step forward using NMT instead of SMT in the automatic post-editing tasks at the Conference on Statistical Machine Translation (WMT16). More recently, Castilho et al. (2017) carried out a more extensive quantitative and qualitative comparative evaluation of PBSMT and NMT using automatic metrics and professional translators. Results were mixed overall. They varied from showing positive results for NMT in terms of improved (perceived) fluency and errors, to achieving no particular gains over SMT at document level for post-editing. While these studies were carried out on better resourced language pairs (English→German, Portuguese, Russian and Greek), they are still highly relevant in indicating the potential impact that the change in MT approaches can have in real-life translation scenarios.

Aside from examining the impact on translator productivity, there has also been increased focus in addressing the shortcomings of NMT, such as those outlined by Koehn and Knowles (2017). As such, a number of innovative approaches have emerged to this end. The application of various transfer learning methods has proven successful for certain low-resourced language (Zoph et al., 2016; Passban et al., 2017), as has the inclusion of linguistic features when addressing data sparsity that faces morphologically rich languages (Sennrich and Haddow, 2016). Luong et al. (2015) show that the use of attention-based NMT can have positive results in many aspects of MT, including the handling of long sentences.

In the case of Irish language, the lack of sufficient data, along with a lack of skilled resources has resulted in limited progress in the area of English-Irish (EN-GA) MT to date: As discussed in Section 1, a domain specific (public administration) SMT system is currently in use by in-house translators in the Department of Culture, Heritage and the Gaeltacht (DCHG) (Dowling et al., 2015). DCHG is the Irish government department responsible for ensuring that the Irish language needs of the Irish public are being met by the government. In addition, some steps have been taken to develop a more broad domain system (Arcan et al., 2016). This current study is, to our knowledge, the first attempt to apply NMT methods to EN-GA MT.

3 Data

In order to provide an accurate comparison in our SMT vs NMT experiments, we use the same data sets for each approach (apart from the absence of monolingual data in the NMT set-up). This data is almost identical to the datasets that we have used in training earlier SMT systems Dowling et al. (2015). We indicate an extended version of a dataset with $\pm$ and our additional datasets with † in Tables 1 and 2.

Bilingual corpora – translation model

Our data sets are based on that of our earlier SMT systems, with some additional corpora. The domain in question is public administration. As Table 1 shows, the majority of the data used to train the translation model was provided by DCHG. These sources include staff notices, annual reports, website content, press releases and official correspondence. We supplement the existing corpus with additional recently translated in-domain data provided by the DCHG. Parallel texts from two EU bodies: the Digital Corpus of the European Parliament (DCEP) and Directorate General for Translation, Translation Memories (DGT-TM) are included in the training data (referred to collectively as 'EU' in Table 1). In addition, we include data crawled from websites[5] that were deemed to contain text from a domain similar to public administration (using the ILSP Focused Crawler (Papavassiliou et al., 2013)). Finally, we contribute a new parallel corpus, which was collected from Conradh na Gaeilge (CnaG), an Irish language organisation which promotes the Irish language in Ireland.

Monolingual data – language model

SMT engines require additional monolingual data in order to train a language model that helps to improve the fluency of the SMT output. This monolingual data does not necessarily need to be in-domain, and thus our language model is trained not only on the GA data used for the translation model, but also on a combination of two additional out-of-domain data sets: 'Paradocs', a corpus of national and European legal texts from `www.gaois.ie` and digital GA content we recently sourced from The University Times (UT)[6].

Data–set	# of words (EN)	# of words (GA)	# of sentences	% proportion
DCHG±	995,419	1,094,707	66,214	60.86%
EU	439,262	483,149	29,445	27.06%
Crawled	213,054	234,028	11,770	10.81%
CnaG†	20,692	21,365	1,367	1.25%
TOTAL	**1,668,427**	**1,833,249**	**108,796**	**100%**

Table 1: Size and distribution of translation model training data.

[5] `www.citizensinfo.ie` (An Irish government website that provides information on public services) and `www.teagasc.ie` (Website for the state agency providing research, advisory and education in agriculture, horticulture, food and rural development in Ireland)

[6] The University Times is a university newspaper in Trinity College Dublin

Data–set	# of words	# of sentences
Paradocs	1,596,569	98,758
UT†	15,377	598

Table 2: Additional monolingual (GA) text used for training the SMT language model

4 Experiment Set–Up

4.1 SMT

To attain the most up-to-date results for this use-case, we train a phrase-based SMT system using Moses (Koehn et al., 2007) with the training data described in Section 3. Earlier findings showed that a 6-gram language model helps address divergent word order in EN-GA (Dowling et al., 2015). We therefore use KenLM (Heafield, 2011) to train a 6-gram language model with the monolingual data outlined in table 1. In addition, we implement hierarchical re-ordering tables to address issues surrounding word order. Our earlier system was tailored to address some consistent errors that arose from data sparsity, which resulted from inflectional variations. We took steps to reduce the repetitive task of the translator in correcting these slight orthographic changes at the token level. Our approach involved the introduction of an automated post-editing (APE) module in the pipeline, which consists of hand-coded grammar rules (Dowling et al., 2016). In order to maximise consistency with our previous work, we chose to include this APE module in our MT experiments.

4.2 NMT

Baseline

In order to provide a preliminary NMT baseline for EN-GA in this domain, we implement a 'vanilla' NMT system, i.e. using default parameters where possible (this system is referred to as NMT-base in Figure 1). We use OpenNMT (Klein et al., 2017), which is an implementation of the popular NMT approach that uses an attentional encoder-decoder network (Bahdanau et al., 2014). We train a 2-layer LSTM with 500 hidden layers for 13 epochs. For the sake of comparison we use the same training data as used in the SMT system (see Table 1). The resulting vocabulary size is 50,002 (English) and 50,004 (Irish). Note that we also apply the APE module to the output of the NMT system.

Further NMT experiments

To add to this baseline system, we also perform a few preliminary experiments to investigate the affect that altering parameters or using other methods would have on an EN-GA NMT system.

- **NMT-250** One such experiment involves experimenting with the number of hidden layers in our NMT system. We implement a smaller model i.e. reduced the number of hidden states from 500 to 250. The results for this system are presented in Table 3 wherein this system is referred to as 'NMT-250'.

- **NMT+ADAM** We also experiment with implementing the stochastic gradient descent with 'Adam', a method for stochastic optimisation (Kinga and Adam, 2015). This method computes individual adaptive learning rates for different parameters from estimates of first and second moments of the gradients. We implement this method using the recommended learning rate for Adam (0.001) and denote this system in Table 3 as NMT+ADAM.

- **NMT+BPE** In order to address the inflectional nature of the Irish language, we experiment with the use of byte-pair encoding (BPE). BPE is a technique presented by Gage (1994) and adapted for NMT by Sennrich et al. (2016b). In terms of MT, it aims to increase vocabulary coverage by encoding rare and unknown words as sequences of subword units. As data sparsity is an issue especially relevant to a low-resourced inflectional language such as Irish, reducing out of vocabulary (OOV) words is a promising technique. This system is referred to as NMT+BPE in Table 3 and Figure 1.

5 Results and Preliminary Analysis

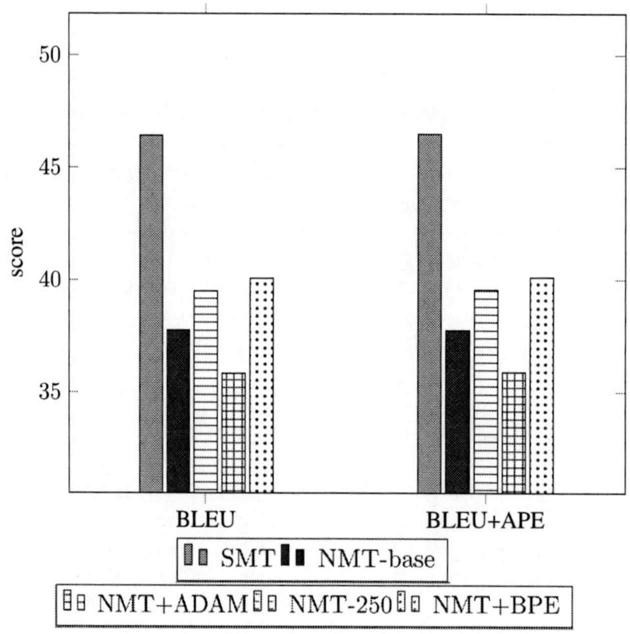

Figure 1: Bar graph displaying the BLEU scores of the SMT and NMT systems, with and without the APE module applied.

Both the SMT and NMT systems were tested on the same test set that were used in earlier experiments (Dowling et al., 2015, 2016), consisting of 1,500 in–domain sentences randomly selected and set aside from the bilingual corpus.

	BLEU	+APE	TER	+APE
SMT	46.44	**46.51**	**43.31**	43.32
NMT	37.77	37.76	47.94	47.79
NMT+ADAM	39.51	39.56	46.98	46.81
NMT-250	35.85	35.9	50.18	50.02
NMT+BPE	40.09	40.11	46.73	46.72

Table 3: BLEU scores for SMT and NMT EN-GA systems before and after applying the automated post-editing module. The highest BLEU score and lowest TER score are highlighted in bold.

We present our results in Table 3 and Figure 1. The results show that for our EN→GA use case, an out-of-the-box NMT system can establish a respectable baseline of BLEU 38.04 and TER 47.94. However, it does not achieve the same level of quality of our tailored SMT system (showing a decrease of between 8.4 and 8.75 BLEU – see Figure 1). Some alterations proved beneficial - the use of Adam as a stochastic optimisation method sees the NMT output increase in BLEU score, and the use of BPE shows an even more marked improvement. Despite these advancements, the scores are still not reaching the same quality as the SMT system.

With respect to the NMT-250 experiment, the use of 250 hidden states in lieu of 500 sees a decrease in BLEU score. More testing will be necessary to identify the optimal number of hidden states for EN-GA NMT.

We note that when the APE module is applied to the NMT output, we see very little change in BLEU score, which is in line with the trends for SMT. However, it should be noted that sentence level analysis carried out in earlier work revealed that the BLEU score increase did not always represent better quality translation from a post-editing perspective (Dowling et al., 2016). This prompts us to carry out some investigation in this regard.

5.1 Sentence-level BLEU

In order to gain a preliminary insight into specific differences between EN-GA SMT and NMT, we chose to perform a sentence-level BLEU on our SMT output and NMT-base output. In Examples 1–4, we highlight some instances where SMT out-performs NMT, and vice-versa.

(1) ***Source:*** Islands[7]
Irish reference: na hOileáin .
SMT: na hOileáin .
NMT: Oileáin .

(NMT decrease: -69.67 BLEU)

(2) ***Source:*** when a requester agrees to amend a request that s / he has submitted , the date of receipt of the refined request is deemed to be the date of receipt of the FOI request .
Irish reference: nuair a chomhaontaíonn iarrthóir leasú a dhéanamh ar iarratas a chuir sé / sí isteach , glacfar leis gurb ionann dáta faighte an iarratais leasaithe agus dáta faighte an iarratais ar SF .
SMT: nuair a chomhaontaíonn iarrthóir leasú a dhéanamh ar iarratas a chuir sé / sí isteach , an dáta faighte an iarratais leasaithe a bheidh an dáta faighte an iarratais SF .
NMT: nuair a aontaíonn iarrthóir iarratas ar iarratas a leasú , meastar go bhfuil an t-iarratas faighte faighte ag an iarrthóir a bheith faighte .

(NMT decrease: -41.56 BLEU)

(3) ***Source:*** this also assists any possible reviews .
Irish reference: Cabhraíonn sé seo le haon athbhreithniú féideartha chomh maith .
SMT: tacaíonn aon athbhreithnithe féideartha seo freisin .
NMT: cabhraíonn sé seo freisin le haon athbhreithniú féideartha .

(NMT increase: +51.62)

(4) ***Source:*** more about CentenaryMayo.ie :
Irish reference: tuilleadh eolais faoi CentenaryMayo.ie :
SMT: níos mó faoi CentenaryMayo.ie :

[7] This is a single word heading.

NMT: tuilleadh faoi CentenaryMayo.ie :

(NMT increase: +35.0)

In Example 1, the SMT BLEU score is significantly higher than that of the NMT output. Delving into the translations, we can see that grammatically, NMT has correctly translated the source text (*Oileáin* 'Islands'). However, the SMT system correctly translates 'Islands' as *na hOileáin*, which literally translates as '*the* Islands'. In this domain, within the context of public administration, it is standard for 'Islands' to refer to the proper noun string '**The** Islands (of Ireland)'. This example highlights the value of a fixed domain, especially for low-resource MT.

Example 2 shows the translation of a longer sentence. It is clear, even to those unfamiliar with the Irish language, why the SMT output prevails in this case. The first phrase in this example is translated perfectly, when compared to the reference – meaning that it is likely that this exact phrase or very similar phrases are present in the training data, and the SMT system is therefore well-equipped to translate it. Looking at the NMT output we can see that a phenomenon, not uncommon in NMT, has occurred: the translations for 'request' and 'receipt' are repeated unnecessarily (*'iarratas'* and *'faighte'*). This is sometimes referred to as 'over-translation' (Tu et al., 2016) and can pose problems for NMT quality.

Examples 3 and 4 show cases where NMT produces translations with a higher BLEU score than that of the SMT system. In Example 3, NMT outputs a more accurate verb (*cabhraíonn* 'assists') as opposed to the SMT output (*tacaíonn* 'supports'), and in fact achieves an almost perfect translation (*freisin* 'also' being a synonym for *chomh maith* 'as well'). It also chooses the correct inflection for *haon* 'any', which the SMT system fails to do (outputting *aon*). The *h* inflection is required following the vowel ending on the preceding preposition *le* 'with'. In Example 4, we again see NMT achieving an almost perfect translation. The translation generated by the SMT system in this case is not entirely incorrect. However, it could be argued that the NMT output is more fluent. Both of these examples highlight the strength in fluency sometimes observed with NMT.

6 Conclusion and Future Work

Our study reveals that an out-of-the-box NMT system, trained on the same EN–GA data, achieves a much lower translation quality than a tailored SMT system, at least in terms of automatic metrics. These results are not necessarily surprising given that Irish presents many of the known challenges that NMT currently struggles with (data scarcity, long sentences and rich morphology). Despite this, these preliminary experiments cannot suggest that NMT be discounted with respect to the future of EN-GA MT. it should be noted that minimal tuning and additional processing has been carried out to date.

In future experiments, we hope to investigate methods for tailoring NMT to this particular domain and language pair. A possible avenue of research to explore is the inclusion of linguistic features in NMT such as the work carried out by Sennrich and Haddow (2016). We wish to address over-translation issues discussed in Section 5, possibly with the use of coverage vectors (Tu et al., 2016). Another approach worth considering is addressing the divergent word order in the EN-GA language pair with a pre-reordering approach such as the one taken by Du and Way (2017). Methods which address data sparsity will also be investigated – options include the use of back translation (Sennrich et al., 2016a) and/or data augmentation (Fadaee et al., 2017).

In addition, it will be important in the future to include human evaluation in our studies to ensure that the MT systems designed for public administration use will be optimised to enhance the task of a human translator, and will not merely be tuned to automatic metrics.

Finally, the derogation on the production of Irish language documents within the EU is due to lift in 2021. By this point there will be a huge increase in the (already high) EN↔GA translation demands, and national and EU bodies will need look to technological advancements to support professional EN↔GA translators. It is vital, therefore, that MT resources are well-developed, up-to-date and designed accordingly to meet this demand.

Acknowledgments

This work was part-funded by the Department of Culture, Heritage and the Gaeltacht (DCHG) and is also supported by the ADAPT Centre for Digital Content Technology, which is funded under the SFI Research Centres Programme (Grant 13/RC/2016) and is co-funded by the European Regional Development Fund. We would also like to thank the four anonymous reviewers for their useful comments.

References

Arcan, M., Lane, C., Droighneáin, E. O., and Buitelaar, P. (2016). Iris: English-Irish machine translation system. In *The International Conference on Language Resources and Evaluation*.

Arenas, A. G. (2008). Productivity and quality in the post-editing of outputs from translation memories and machine translation. *Localisation Focus*, 7(1):11–21.

Bahdanau, D., Cho, K., and Bengio, Y. (2014). Neural machine translation by jointly learning to align and translate. *CoRR*, abs/1409.0473.

Bentivogli, L., Bisazza, A., Cettolo, M., and Federico, M. (2016). Neural versus phrase-based machine translation quality: a case study. In *Proceedings of the 2016 Conference on Empirical Methods in NaturalLanguage Processing*, pages 257–267. Association for Computational Linguistics.

Bojar, O., Chatterjee, R., Federmann, C., Graham, Y., Haddow, B., Huck, M., Jimeno Yepes, A., Koehn, P., Logacheva, V., Monz, C., Negri, M., Neveol, A., Neves, M., Popel, M., Post, M., Rubino, R., Scarton, C., Specia, L., Turchi, M., Verspoor, K., and Zampieri, M. (2016). Findings of the 2016 conference on machine translation. In *Proceedings of the First Conference on Machine Translation: Volume 2, Shared Task Papers*, pages 131–198. Association for Computational Linguistics.

Castilho, S., Moorkens, J., Gaspari, F., Sennrich, R., Sosoni, V., Georgakopoulou, Y., Lohar, P., Way, A., Miceli Barone, A. V., and Gialama, M. (2017). A Comparative Quality Evaluation of PBSMT and NMT using Professional Translators. In *Proceedings of Machine Translation Summit XVI*, Nagoya, Japan.

Dowling, M., Cassidy, L., Maguire, E., Lynn, T., Srivastava, A., and Judge, J. (2015). Tapadóir: Developing a statistical machine translation engine and associated resources for Irish. In *Proceedings of the The Fourth LRL Workshop: "Language Technologies in support of Less-Resourced Languages"*, Poznan, Poland.

Dowling, M., Lynn, T., Graham, Y., and Judge, J. (2016). English to Irish machine translation with automatic post-editing. *PARIS Inalco du 4 au 8 juillet 2016*, page 42.

Du, J. and Way, A. (2017). Pre-reordering for neural machine translation: Helpful or harmful? *The Prague Bulletin of Mathematical Linguistics*, 108(1):171–182.

Etchegoyhen, T., Bywood, L., Fishel, M., Georgakopoulou, P., Jiang, J., van Loenhout, G., del Pozo, A., Maucec, M. S., Turner, A., and Volk, M. (2014). Machine translation for subtitling: a large-scale evaluation. In *Proceedings of theNinth International Conference on Language Resources and Evaluation*.

Fadaee, M., Bisazza, A., and Monz, C. (2017). Data augmentation for low-resource neural machine translation. In *Proceedings of the 55th Annual Meeting of the Association for Computational Linguistics (Volume 2: Short Papers)*, volume 2, pages 567–573.

Gage, P. (1994). A new algorithm for data compression. *The C Users Journal*, 12(2):23–38.

Heafield, K. (2011). Kenlm: Faster and smaller language model queries. In *Proceedings of the Sixth Workshop on Statistical Machine Translation*, pages 187–197. Association for Computational Linguistics.

Kinga, D. and Adam, J. B. (2015). Adam: A method for stochastic optimization. In *International Conference on Learning Representations (ICLR)*.

Klein, G., Kim, Y., Deng, Y., Senellart, J., and Rush, A. (2017). Opennmt: Open-source toolkit for neural machine translation. *Proceedings of the 55th Annual Meeting of the Association of Computational Linguistics 2017, System Demonstrations*, pages 67–72.

Koehn, P., Hoang, H., Birch, A., Callison-Burch, C., Federico, M., Bertoldi, N., Cowan, B., Shen, W., Moran, C., Zens, R., et al. (2007). Moses: Open source toolkit for statistical machine translation. In *Proceedings of the 45th annual meeting of the ACL on interactive poster and demonstration sessions*, pages 177–180. Association for Computational Linguistics.

Koehn, P. and Knowles, R. (2017). Six challenges for neural machine translation. In *Proceedings of the First Workshop on Neural Machine Translation*, pages 28–39.

Luong, T., Pham, H., and Manning, C. D. (2015). Effective approaches to attention-based neural machine translation. In *Proceedings of the 2015 Conference on Empirical Methods in Natural Language Processing*, pages 1412–1421.

Papavassiliou, V., Prokopidis, P., and Thurmair, G. (2013). A modular open-source focused crawler for mining monolingual and bilingual corpora from the web. In *Proceedings of the Sixth Workshop on Building and Using Comparable Corpora*, pages 43–51, Sofia, Bulgaria. Association for Computational Linguistics.

Passban, P., Liu, Q., and Way, A. (2017). Translating low-resource languages by vocabulary adaptation from close counterparts. *ACM Transactions on Asian and Low-Resource Language Information Processing (TALLIP)*, 16(4):29.

Sennrich, R. and Haddow, B. (2016). Linguistic input features improve neural machine translation. In *Proceedings of the First Conference on Machine Translation: Volume 1, Research Papers*, volume 1, pages 83–91.

Sennrich, R., Haddow, B., and Birch, A. (2016a). Improving neural machine translation models with monolingual data. In *Proceedings of the 54th Annual Meeting of the Association for Computational Linguistics (Volume 1: Long Papers)*, volume 1, pages 86–96.

Sennrich, R., Haddow, B., and Birch, A. (2016b). Neural machine translation of rare words with subword units. In *Proceedings of the 54th Annual Meeting of the Association for Computational Linguistics (Volume 1: Long Papers)*, volume 1, pages 1715–1725.

Tu, Z., Lu, Z., Liu, Y., Liu, X., and Li, H. (2016). Modeling coverage for neural machine translation. In *Proceedings of the 54th Annual Meeting of the Association for Computational Linguistics (Volume 1: Long Papers)*, volume 1, pages 76–85.

Zoph, B., Yuret, D., May, J., and Knight, K. (2016). Transfer learning for low-resource neural machine translation. In *Proceedings of the 2016 Conference on Empirical Methods in Natural Language Processing*, pages 1568–1575.

Tibetan-Chinese Neural Machine Translation based on Syllable Segmentation

Wen Lai Lavine_Lai@126.com
National Language Resource Monitoring & Research Center of Minority Languages, Minzu University of China, Beijing, 100081, China
Xiaobing Zhao* nmzxb_cn@163.com
National Language Resource Monitoring & Research Center of Minority Languages, Minzu University of China, Beijing, 100081, China
Wei Bao wei.bao@adaptcentre.ie
National Language Resource Monitoring & Research Center of Minority Languages, Minzu University of China, Beijing, 100081, China

Abstract

Machine translation is one of the important research directions in natural language processing. In recent years, neural machine translation methods have surpassed traditional statistical machine translation methods in translation performance of most of language and have become the mainstream methods of machine translation. In this paper, we proposed syllable segmentation in Tibetan translation tasks for the first time and achieved better results than Tibetan word segmentation. Four kinds of neural machine translation methods, which are influential in recent years, are compared and analyzed in Tibetan-Chinese corpus. Experimental results showed that the translation model based on the complete self-attention mechanism performed best in the translation task of Tibetan-Chinese corpus, and performance of the most of the neural machine translation methods surpassed performance of the traditional statistical machine translation methods.

Key words: Tibetan-Chinese translation; Neural machine translation; Syllabe Segmentation

1. Introduction

Machine translation, studies on how to use computers to achieve the automatic translation between natural languages, is one of the important research directions in areas of artificial intelligence and natural language processing (Liu, 2017). Natural language processing (including machine translation) is a discipline that crosses computer science and linguistics. Based on characteristics of this discipline, the system of machine translation can be divided into two categories, which are the rule-based methods and the corpus-based methods. Among them, corpus-based methods can be divided into statistics-based methods and example-based methods (Zhao et al., 2000). In recent years, with the development of internet technology, machine translation has achieved fruitful results both in academia and industry.

Since the advent of the neural network in the 1940s, it has experienced the different stages of rising, low tide, and rising. Until 2006, Hinton et al. solved the historic problem of neural networks (Hinton et al., 2006), and the related researches of deep learning and neural network returned to people's attention again. Since then, with the deepening of theoretical research and improvement of computing speed of computers, neural networks have been gradually applied to various fields of artificial intelligence and have made major breakthroughs. Researches about natural language processing have also made a rapid progress along with this tide.

In 2012, With the Hinton research group participated in the ImageNet image recognition contest and won the championship, which opened the prelude of deep learning in the big bang in various fields of artificial intelligence. Neural machine translation (NMT) is also a machine translation method that is gradually emerging at this stage. The main processes of neural machine translation are as follows: Firstly, it uses neural networks (RNN, CNN, etc.) to encode the source language into word embedding. Secondly, the word-embedding generates the target language by decoding . Among them, in the neural network training, the problem of long distance dependence can be solved well by the proper joining of long-short term memory (LSTM) networks and attention mechanisms.

Tibetan is a kind of pinyin character, and its syllables are composed of 34 vowel consonants, then Tibetan words are composed of syllables (Wei, 2015). A single character in a Tibetan text is a unit, and it is separated by a syllable separator "་" between words (Cai, 2016). Based on the characteristics of Tibetan language, at present, the statistical machine translation model is mainly used in the research on Tibetan translation model, and the relevant theoretical research has basically stopped at the stage of word processing and other corpus preprocessing such as the phrase-based Tibetan-Chinese statistical machine translation system (Dong et al., 2012); besides, related tibetan preprocessing research (Hua, 2014; Wang, 2016; Wan et al., 2015) and so on. On the whole, compared with research on machine translation of other rich languages, the research on Tibetan-Chinese machine translation is obviously behind. There are few researches on using neural network model in Tibetan corpus (Li et al., 2017). Tibetan texts are all word segmentation pre-processed in traditional Tibetan machine translations (Guan, 2015). In this article, the traditional method of Tibetan word segmentation is completely abandoned, and Tibetan texts are directly divided by syllables. It gets a better performance than Tibetan word segmentation.

In this paper, four kinds of influential machine translation models of neural networks are applied to the task of Tibetan-Chinese machine translation, and the final translation results are analyzed in detail. The experimental results show that the application of neural network machine translation model on Tibetan-Chinese machine translation has basically surpassed the performance of the traditional statistical machine translation model. By using the method of syllable segmentation in Tibetan machine translation tasks, it has a better translation performance than the method of word segmentation.

2. Neural Network Machine Translation Models

2.1. Seq2Seq

The Seq2Seq model is a sequence-to-sequence model. In many translation models in the past, a feature matrix was input during training, and each input corresponds to a row in the matrix. Therefore, these rows have the same dimension, which is not in accordance with the task of machine translation. Because, for machine translation tasks, we cannot guarantee that every sentence you input has the same number of words. Conversely, the input of the Seq2Seq model is a sequence, and the output is also a sequence. The length of the input sequence and the output sequence of this model is variable, which is the biggest difference between this model and the previous neural mahine translation model.

The Seq2Seq model was presented in 2014, and two articles published by the Google Brain team (Ilya et al., 2014) and the Yoshua Bengio team (Cho et al., 2014) illustrate the basic idea of the model. The basic idea of solving the problem of the Seq2Seq model is to map an input sequence to an output sequence through one or more deep neural network models, which commonly known as LSTM --- Long short-term memories network (D'Informatique et al., 2001), and this process consists of two parts of encoding input and decoding output.

In the encoder section, an input sequence X will be compiled into a vector C via an encoder built with recurrent neural networks (RNNs). The vector C is usually the last hidden node in the RNN, or the weighted sum of multiple hidden nodes.

In the decoder section, vector C will be decoded by the RNN decoder. The decoding process can be simply understood as using a series of algorithms to return the word with the highest probability corresponding to the input vector to get the optimal output sequence.

2.2. RNNSearch

In 2015, RNNSearch machine translation model was proposed by Bahdanau et al. (Bahdanau et al., 2014). This model adds the attention mechanism to the encoder-decoder structure, and the translation performance is greatly enhanced. In this model the attention mechanism is also used in natural language processing tasks for the first time.

The Attention mechanism is added into the translation model, which breaks the limitation that the traditional encoder-decoder structure, such as Seq2Seq model, relies on a fixed length vector in the process of decoding. The attention mechanism is achieved by preserving the intermediate output results of the input sequence encoded by the encoder and then retraining a new model to selectively learn these input sequences and associate the output sequence with the output of the model. In machine translation tasks, the model using the attention mechanism generates a word vector every time, and it finds one of the most relevant word sets in the input sequence, and then the model will predict the next target word generate based on the current context vectors and all previous generated words to achieve the best translation results.

2.3. Fairseq

Fairseq machine translation model was presented by the Facebook team in May 2017 (Gehring, 2017). The traditional method of sequence to sequence learning is to map an input sequence to a variable length output sequence through one or more layers of RNN neural network. The Fairseq model introduces an architecture based entirely on convolutional neural networks (CNNs). Compared with the recurrent neural network model, all calculations of the element sequence of Fairseq model in training are completely parallel, the number of nonlinear sequences is fixed and independent of the length of the input sequence.

An important part of the Fairseq model in model structure is the multihop attention mechanism. The multihop alert mechanism is an enhanced version of attentional mechanics that allows the neural network to scan sentence sequences more often to produce better results and to influence each scan. Another important part of the model is the gating, which controls the flow of information in a neural network. Sentence sequences are transmitted downward through hidden units in a neural network, and the gating mechanism is used to precisely control the sequence information passed to the next unit, and the translation effect is greatly improved.

The research shows that in the same environment, the training time of Fairseq model is 9 times faster than the translation model based on RNN network, and its accuracy is also higher than that of the model based on RNN network.

2.4. Transformer

Transformer machine translation model was proposed by the Google team in June 2017 (Vaswani et al. 2017). Neural network is mostly used as the model basis of Encoder-Decoder in traditional neural network machine translation model. This model is based on the attention mechanism and completely abandons the inherent model of the neural machine translation model without any neural network (CNN or RNN) structure. Experiments show that this model can run in parallel and greatly improve the speed of model training while improving machine translation performance.

Transformer model requires only a small number of uninterrupted steps in the training process, at each step, it uses a self-note mechanism that can directly relate to all words in the sentence and the location of each word does not need to be considered, and model efficiency is also greatly enhanced while simplifying the model. Besides the improvement of computational performance and higher semantic understanding, the transformer model also provides a visual display of how words are processed and how the information travels across the network.

Transformer model performs well in natural language processing tasks such as syntax analysis and semantic understanding, which is also a systematic breakthrough for natural language processing communities over decades.

3. Experimental Setup

3.1. Experimental corpus

This paper uses the evaluation corpus of the 13th National machine translation symposium(CWMT 2017 in china, http://ee.dlut.edu.cn/CWMT2017/index.html). These corpora are processed into Tibetan-Chinese sentence pairs, which contains word segmentation, syllable segmentation and some alignment process. These corpora are shown in following Table 1.

Table 1 Experimental Corpus

Corpus	Department	Corpus-Area	Scale (sentence pairs)
QHNU-CWMT2013	Qinghai Normal University (in China)	Government	33145
QHNU-CWMT2015	Qinghai Normal University (in China)	Government	17194
XBMU-XMU	Artificial intelligence institute of XiaMen University (in China) Institute of language (technology), Northwestern University of Nationalities (in China)	Synthesize	52078
XBMU-XMU-UTibent	Institute of language (technology), Northwestern University of Nationalities (in China) Tibet University Artificial intelligence institute of XiaMen University (in China)	Government Law	24159
ICT-TC-Corpus	Institute of Computing Technology, Chinese Academy of Sciences (in China)	News	30004

3.2. Corpus preprocessing

In this paper, Tibetan-Chinese bilingual parallel corpus is pre-processed and then divided into a training set, (141601 sentence pairs), a development set (1000 sentence pairs) and a test set

(1000 sentence pairs). Pre-processing tasks include: word segmentation of the Tibetan corpus, character segmentation, and operation on word segmentation of the Chinese corpus. Details are shown as Table2.

Table 2 Corpus Statistics in Experimental

Language	Sentence pairs	Words	Characters
Tibetan	141601	16547	13701
Chinese	141601	23644	4968

3.3. Experimental setting

In the experiment, in order to reflect the performance of neural machine translation, phrase-based statistical machine translation model Nitutrans (Xiao T et al., 2012) developed by natural language processing laboratory in northeastern university (in china) is used in the statistical machine translation model. In this paper, four models of neural machine translation are consistent in the basic parameter settings (the vocabulary size of sub-words is set to 32000 and the number of training iterations is 200000). Because each model has its own architecture, it is difficult to achieve consistent in terms of performance of parameters. In addition, with the language characteristics of the Tibetan-Chinese bilingual corpus, in this paper, based on each model, hyperparameters are adjusted to achieve maximum of translation performance. Bilingual evaluation understudy (BLEU) is used as evaluation index in this paper (Papineni, 2007).

4. Experimental Results

4.1. Corpus according to Character segmentation and word segmentation

In order to verify the effect of the character segmentation (Tibetan syllables segmentation and Chinese characters segmentation) and the word segmentation (Tibetan word segmentation and Chinese word segmentation) of Tibetan corpus on the translation performance, Syllable segmentation and Tibetan word segmentation of Tibetan-Chinese bilingual parallel corpus was conducted on the basis of the transformer model in the experiment. Among them, Tibetan word segmentation tool TIP-LAS is used in the Tibetan word segmentation (Li et al., 2015). THU-LAC software opened by Tsinghua university is used to conduct Chinese word segmentation (Li et al., 2009). The experimental results of Tibetan-Chinese machine translation are shown in table 3. The experimental results of Chinese-Tibetan machine are shown in table 4.

Table 3 Corpus according to Character segmentation and word segmentation (Tibetan-Chinese)

Model	Corpus processing	BLEU
Transformer	Character	51.38
Transformer	Word	38.44

Table 4 Corpus according to Character segmentation and word segmentation (Chinese-Tibetan)

Model	Corpus processing	BLEU
Transformer	Character	41.00
Transformer	Word	30.94

The experimental results show that in neural machine translation, whether Tibetan is translated into Chinese or Chinese is translated into Tibetan, the effect of Character segmentation on corpus is obviously higher than that of word segmentation on corpus. This is the biggest difference between traditional machine translation corpus processing and machine translation corpus processing in this paper.

4.2. BPE impacting

The problems of OOV (out of vocabulary) in neural machine translation and Rare Words are usually solved by back-off dictionaries. In 2016, Sennrich et al. (Sennrich, 2015) attempted a more simple and effective way (Subword Units) to represent open vocabularies inspired by translation strategies of the same root word, compound word, naming entity, and foreign language. He considered that separating these rare words into a combination of "subword units" effectively alleviate the problem of translating OOV and rare words. The segmentation strategy of subword unit here draws on a data compression algorithm: Byte Pair Encoding (BPE) algorithm (Suarjaya, 2012; Shibata et al., 1999). In order to verify whether the corpus needs to be pre-processed by BPE before Tibetan-Chinese translation, we have a comparation between BPE processing and no BPE processing. The experimental results are shown in Table 5.

Table 5 BPE impacting (Tibetan-Chinese)

Model	BPE	Corpus processing	BLEU
Transformer	Yes	Character	51.38
Transformer	No	Character	48.50

The experimental results show that in the neural machine translation model, the translation effect will be improved when using BPE processing.

4.3. Different Neural Networks with the Same Structure

In order to verify the performance of different neural networks with the same model structure, experiments were conducted in RNNSearch and Fairseq models respectively. Both RNNSearch and Fairseq models are models based on the neural network and attention mechanism. The only difference is that RNNSearch is a model based on cyclic neural networks, whereas Fairseq is a model based on convolutional neural networks. The experimental results are shown in Table 6.

Table 6 Different Neural Networks with the Same Structure (Tibetan-Chinese)

Model	Network	Corpus processing	BLEU
RNNSearch	RNN	Character	45.63
Fairseq	CNN	Character	46.94

The experimental results show that there are obvious differences in the translation performance for different neural networks models with the same model structure, and because of its characteristics of the model based on CNN, training time greatly reduced and performance exceeds RNN-based neural network model.

4.4. Different Neural Machine Translation Models in Tibetan-Chinese Corpus

In order to verify the performance of different neural machine translation models on Tibetan-Chinese translation, training of Tibetan-Chinese machine translation model was carried out in four different neural network models respectively in this experiment, meanwhile, the same corpus was trained in statistical machine translation model. Machine translation model Niutrans opened by the natural language processing laboratory of Northeastern University(in china) is used in the statistical machine translation model (use Chinese as monolingual data). The experimental results are shown in Table 7.

Table 7 Different Neural Machine Translation Models in Tibetan - Chinese Corpus (Tibetan-Chinese)

Model	Framework	Corpus processing	BLEU
Niutrans	Phrased-based	character	26.98
		word	24.35
Seq2Seq	RNN	character	32.16
		word	22.19
RNNSearch	RNN+Attention	character	32.16
		word	29.21
Fairseq	CNN+Attention	character	46.94
		word	31.66
Transformer	Attention	character	51.38
		word	38.44

The experimental results show that there are obvious differences in the translation performance of different neural machine translation models. Among them, Most neural machine translation models have better translation performance than statistical machine translation models; translation performance of the model Transformer based on complete self-attention mechanism is the best; the same machine translation model, translation performance of character-based processing is better than performance of word segmentation processing; training time of Fairseq model is the fastest.

5. Conclusion

In this paper, the four-influential neural machine translation models: the Seq2Seq model based on the RNN, the RNNSearch model based on RNN+Attention mechanism, the Fairseq model based on CNN + Attention mechanism, and the Transformer model based on self-attention mechanism are compared in Tibetan-Chinese machine translation tasks. Through the comparison, it has the following findings:

1. In Tibetan translation task, most of the translation performance of the machine translation model of neural network is better traditional statistical machine translation model;
2. In the Tibetan translation (Tibetan-Chinese, Chinese-Tibetan) task, the translation performance of character processing on the original corpus (Tibetan syllable segmentation, Chinese word segmentation) is better than that of word segmentation processing on the corpus;
3. In the neural machine translation model, BPE processing on the original corpus can optimize the translation performance;
4. Different neural network with the same structure, the translation performance of CNN-based neural network is better than the translation performance of RNN-based neural network, and the training speed of CNN-based machine translation model of neural network is much faster than that of RNN-based machine translation model of neural network;
5. The translation performance of the Transformer model based on the completely self-attention mechanism is the best in Tibetan translation tasks.

Acknowledgement

This work is supported by the National Science Foundation of China (61331013).

References

Bahdanau, Dzmitry, Kyunghyun. Cho, and Yoshua. Bengio. "Neural Machine Translation by Jointly Learning to Align and Translate." *Computer Science* (2014).

Cai, Zhijie and Cai, Rangzhuoma. " Research on the Distribution of Tibetan Character Forms." *Journal of Chinese Information Processing* 30.4(2016):98-105. (in Chinese)

Cho, Kyunghyun, Van Merrienboer, Bart, Gulcehre, Caglar, Bahdanau, Dzmitry, Bougares, Fethi, Schwenk, Holger and Bengio, Yoshua. "Learning Phrase Representations using RNN Encoder-Decoder for Statistical Machine Translation." *Computer Science* (2014).

Dong, Xiaofang, Cao, Hui, and Jiang, tao. " Phrase Based Tibetan - Chinese Statistical Machine Translation System." *Technology Wind* 17(2012):60-61. (in Chinese)

Gers, Felix. "Long short-term memory in recurrent neural networks." Unpublished PhD dissertation, *Ecole Polytechnique Fédérale de Lausanne*, Lausanne, Switzerland (2001).

Guan, Queduojie. "Research on Tibetan Segmentation for Machine Translation." *electronic test* 22(2015):46-48. (in Chinese)

Gehring, Jonas, Auli, Michael, Grangier, David, Yarats, Denis, and Dauphin, Yann N. "Convolutional Sequence to Sequence Learning." (2017).

Hinton, Geoffrey E., Simon Osindero, and Yee-Whye Teh. "A fast learning algorithm for deep belief nets." *Neural computation* 18.7 (2006): 1527-1554.

Hua, Guocairang. " Tibetan Verb Researching in Chinese Tibetan Machine Translation." Diss. *Qinghai Normal University* (in china), 2014. (in Chinese)

Liu, Yang. "Recent Advances in Neural Machine Translation." *Journal of Computer Research and Development* 54.6(2017):1144-1149. (in Chinese)

Li, Yachao, Xiong, Deyi, Zhang, Min, Jiang, Jing, Ma, Ning and Yin, Jianmin. " Research on Tibetan-Chinese Neural Machine Translation." *Journal of Chinese Information Processing* 31.6 (2017): 103-109. (in Chinese)

Li, Yachao, Jiang, Jing, Jia, Yangji and Yu, Hongzhi. "TIP-LAS: An Open Source Toolkit for Tibetan Word Segmentation and Part of Speech Tagging." *Journal of Chinese Information Processing* 29.6 (2015): 203-207. (in Chinese)

Li, Zhongguo, and M. Sun. Punctuation as implicit annotations for chinese word segmentation. *MIT Press*, 2009.

Papineni, Kishore, Roukos, Salim, Ward, Todd and Zhu, Weijing. "BLEU: a method for automatic evaluation of machine translation." *Proceedings of the 40th annual meeting on association for computational linguistics*. Association for Computational Linguistics, 2002.

Sutskever, Ilya, Oriol Vinyals, and Quoc V. Le. "Sequence to sequence learning with neural networks." *Advances in neural information processing systems*. 2014.

Sennrich, Rico, Barry, Haddow, and Alexandra, Birch. "Neural Machine Translation of Rare Words with Subword Units." *Computer Science* (2015).

Suarjaya, I. Made Agus Dwi. "A New Algorithm for Data Compression Optimization." *International Journal of Advanced Computer Science & Applications* 3.8(2012).

Shibata, Yusuke, Kida, Takuya, Fukamachi, Shuichi, Takeda, Masayuki, Shinohara, Ayumi, Shinohara, Takeshi and Arikawa, Setsuo. " Byte Pair encoding: A text compression scheme that accelerates pattern matching." Technical Report DOI-TR-161, *Department of Informatics, Kyushu University*, 1999.

Vaswani, Ashish, Shazeer, Noam, Parmar, Niki, Uszkoreit, Jakob, Jones, Llion, Gomez, Aidan N., Kaiser, Lukasz and Polosukhin, Illia. "Attention is all you need." *Advances in Neural Information Processing Systems*. 2017.

Wei, Sudong. " Research on Tibetan - Chinese Online Translation System Based on Phrases." Diss. *Northwest University for Nationalities (in china)*, 2015. (in Chinese)

Wang, Tianhang. " Research on Tibetan Functional Chunk Identification for Machine Translation." Diss. *Beijing Institute of Technology (in china)*, 2016. (in Chinese)

Wan, Fucheng, Yu, Hongzhi, Wu, Xihong and He, Xiangzhen. " Research of Tibetan syntax for machine translation." *Computer Engineering and Applications* 51.13(2015):211-215. (in Chinese)

Xiao, Tong, Zhu, Jingbo, Zhang, Hao and Li, Qiang. "NiuTrans: an open source toolkit for phrase-based and syntax-based machine translation." *50th Meeting of the Association for Computational Linguistics* 2012:19-24.

Zhao Tiejun. Machine Translation Theory. *Harbin Institute of Technology Press*, 1900. (in Chinese)

A Survey of Machine Translation Work in the Philippines: From 1998 to 2018

Nathaniel Oco naoco@national-u.edu.ph
Rachel Edita Roxas reoroxas@national-u.edu.ph
National University, Manila, 1008, Philippines

Abstract

In this paper, we present a survey covering the last 20 years of machine translation work in the Philippines. We detail the various approaches used and innovations applied. We also discuss the various mechanisms and support that keep the MT community thriving, as well as the challenges ahead.

1. Introduction

The Philippines is a country in Southeast Asia with 7,107 islands, and 187 languages – broken down as follows: 175 are indigenous, 8 are non-indigenous, and 4 are already extinct[1]. The official languages are: (1) Filipino, which was based on Tagalog and has 45 million L2 users[2]; and (2) English. Because the country is a gold mine for language data, there is already a thriving Natural Language Processing (NLP) community as evidenced by the existence of the following: the Computing Society of the Philippines – Special Interest Group on Natural Language Processing (CSP SIG-NLP)[3]; various institutions and research laboratories working on NLP[4,5]; venues to share ideas and knowledge like the National NLP Research Symposium (NNLPRS)[6]; and hosting of international conferences such as the 31st Pacific Asia Conference on Language, Information and Computation or PACLIC 31 (2017)[7].

One work (Raga, 2016) looked at the progress of NLP research in the country by reviewing 12 editions of NNLPRS. Our work differs in that we are focused on machine translation and we also looked at other venues. With NNLPRS as starting point, we branched out to cover the references the authors cited, other conference proceedings, journal issues, and works by members of CSP SIG-NLP. We took note of the approaches used, data size, and innovations applied.

The rest of the paper is organized as follows: in section 2, we present the evolution of machine translation in the Philippines by presenting the various approaches used over time; in section 3, we discuss the different innovations applied from data collection to evaluation; we tackle the challenges in section 4; and we conclude our work in section 5.

[1]Data according to Ethnologue: https://www.ethnologue.com/country/PH
[2]Data according to Ethnologue: https://www.ethnologue.com/language/fil
[3]Computing Society of the Philippines: http://csp.org.ph/
[4]National University's Research and Innovation Office: http://www.national-u.edu.ph/?page_id=44
[5]De La Salle University's Center for Language Technologies: http://www.dlsu.edu.ph/research/centers/adric/nlp/
[6]Website of the recently concluded student research workshop organized by CSP SIG-NLP: https://sites.google.com/bicol-u.edu.ph/14nnlprs-pre-conference/home
[7]PACLIC 31 (2017): http://paclic31.national-u.edu.ph/

2. Approaches

Machine translation started in the late '90s covering the two official languages (Roxas et al., 1999): Filipino/Tagalog and English. It later on included other Philippines languages[8] such as Cebuano (Yara, 2007), Kankanaey (Ananayo et al., 2011), Maranao (Dimalen et al., 2009), Hiligaynon (Macabante et al., 2017), Ilocano (Miguel and Dy, 2008; Bautista et al., 2015; Lazaro et al., 2017), and Bicol (Fernandez et al., 2018). Applications of machine translation since then can be grouped into three: (1) in tourism (Lazaro et al., 2017); (2) in translating informational materials such as books for mother tongue-based – multilingual education or MTB-MLE (Oco et al., 2016); and (3) in humanitarian technologies, for example to assist policy makers make sense of community input (Octaviano et al., 2018). We've seen that early works only tackled declarative and imperative statements but the advent of statistical machine translation (Nocon et al., 2014) paved the way to also include interrogative statements. We have observed that all serious research undertaking has been supported in part by government funding. It started with transfer-based approaches and succeeding projects have seen rule-based, corpus-based, statistical, and deep learning approaches. In the succeeding text, we discuss these projects and the approaches used, and direction.

2.1. Transfer-based approaches

Machine translation in the Philippines traces its early roots to transfer-based approaches. One such project is IsaWika! (Roxas et al., 1999), an English-Tagalog machine translator for declarative and imperative sentences, that used an augmented transition network and a dictionary size of less than 10,000 entries. The project's second phase started in 1998 and was funded by the Department of Science and Technology – Philippine Council for Advanced Science and Technology Research and Development (DOST-PCASTRD). This was immediately followed by a project (Borra, 1999) which explored lexical functional grammar or LFG as the grammar formalism. The f-structure and c-structures also showed promise in identifying translation errors. LFG would be a staple in machine translation projects with XLE parser (Frank et al., 1998) as the core. One project (Borra et al., 2007) used a transfer dictionary with 2,000 parallel word pairs while another project (Cada et al., 2012) used a bootstrapping technique to develop a larger parallel corpus from earlier works. Recent developments include the use of a natural language generator called Linguist's Assistant (Allman et al., 2014) to translate religious text[9]. It is being used to build lexicons and grammars in Filipino, Ayta Mag-indi, and Botolan languages, and can be used towards developing materials for mother tongue-based – multilingual education or MTB-MLE (Oco et al., 2016), a form of education where children's mother tongue are used as the primary mode of teaching until primary school. In all transfer-based projects, we have noticed that the corpus size is limited and vocabulary is only within the scope of available resources.

2.2. Corpus-based

Seeing the limitations of manually creating rules in a transfer-based approach, various corpora were soon utilized. After IsaWika!, DOST-PCASTRD funded a hybrid English-Filipino machine translation system from 2005 to 2008 (Roxas, 2006; Roxas et al., 2008). It combined both transfer-based and corpus-based approaches.

---

[8]Both Kankanaey and Maranao are considered indigenous languages

[9]A version of Linguist's Assistant called "The Bible Translator's Assistant" is being used to translate books of the Bible to low-resource Philippine languages. Website: http://www.thebibletranslatorsassistant.org/

The transfer-based approach used an LFG formalism while the corpus-based approaches extracted patterns (Alcantara et al., 2006) from a large document and stored them in templates (Go et al., 2007). The project used a parallel corpus with 207,000 Filipino words and a dictionary with 4,000 words. For hybrid systems, the challenge is integrating results from multiple machine translators. One solution is to develop a module that can provide translation scores.

2.3. Statistical

The Network-based ASEAN Languages Translation Public Service or ASEANMT saw the introduction of statistical approaches. It aims to "*build a practical network-based service on ASEAN languages text translation in the tourism domain. ASEAN languages resources and knowledge of the translation technology are availably shared among ASEAN member states and other countries*"[10]. It is supported by the Association of Southeast Asian Nations Committee on Science and Technology (ASEAN COST). The Center for Language Technologies at De La Salle University represented the country in this project with funding from the Commission on Higher Education for the counterpart system (Ilao et al., 2015; Nocon et al., 2014). Moses engine[11] was used with covering 20,000 sentence pairs on the tourism domain and at least 100,000 thousand sentence pairs derived from Wikipedia articles and manually translated. A demo version is available online[12].

2.4. Directions

We see the direction of machine translation to be heading towards deep learning because of the availability of approaches to automatically build parallel corpora. One work (Tacorda et al., 2017), also supported by government funding[13], utilized RNN with 100,000 pairs of sentences and integrated byte pair encoding (BPE) to reduce out-of-vocabulary errors (OOVs). BPE works by segmenting a token into identifiable sequences. This allowed for tokens not present in the training data to be recognized if its root and affixes have been identified through BPE. The danger is with false positives: character sequences part of the root can be identified falsely as an affix.

Aside from deep learning, recent trends in machine translation focused on its application in humanitarian technologies. As example, one project (Octaviano et al., 2018) is involved in eParticipation, specifically in cross-lingual topic modeling – translating community responses and generating topic models through LDA – to make sense of community inputs. Qualitative evaluation showed cross-lingual topic modeling generated more coherent topic models. Another work (Fernandez et al., 2018) aims at assisting non-linguists in translating questions for survey use.

3. Innovations

Aside from BPE, other innovations to reduce OOVs include the use of domain adaptation techniques (Lazaro et al., 2017) by filtering the training data, and allowing users to provide correction through feedback (Ang et al., 2015). Other projects addressed OOVs by increasing the training data through automatic means. One work (Dimalen and Roxas), crawled the web

[10]Website: http://aseanmt.org/

[11]Website: http://www.statmt.org/moses/

[12]Demo version: http://www.aseanmt.org/mt/

[13]Supported in part by the Philippine Commission on Higher Education through the Philippine-California Advanced Research Institutes Project (no. IIID-2015-07)

and automatically identified the language through a trigram ranking approach. Odds-ratio was applied since closely related languages yield to lower recall rates. Other researchers have attempted to find bilingual pairs of terms (Lat et al., 2006) and sentences (Tabaranza et al., 2016) in comparable corpora. There are also attempts to gamify manual translation (Ilao et al., 2016) in role-playing games: if the user wants to earn more credit points, he/she can translate phrases and there's an automatic scoring mechanism that rewards the user after a given time frame. There are also those (Octaviano et al., 2018) that apply spell checking and language identification as pre-processing step to clean the data. To assist translators, one work (Oco and Borra, 2011) utilized Transifex in localizing labels and instructions. Another allowed linguists to provide semantic representations (Allman et al., 2014).

As for evaluation, the ASEAN MT asked manual annotators to evaluate machine translation output and provide a rating from 1 to 5, with the highest having semantic equivalence with the manually translated one. Another (Allman et al., 2014) asked students to read manually translated and automatically translated materials and an assessment task was given. Those who were given the automatically translated material as reference scored higher than those who were given manually translated materials.

4. Challenges

Aside from free-word order, there are other challenges that make translation work in the Philippines interesting:

- Verbs have both tense and focus (Ramos and Cena, 1990).
- Affixes can be divided into prefix, infix, suffix, circumfixation, and there is also affix reduplication (Schachter and Otanes, 1972).
- Plurality exists in pronouns, modifiers, and verbs (Ramos, 1971; Cubar and Cubar, 1994; Kroeger, 1993).

5. Conclusion

We have surveyed projects covering the last 20 years of machine translation work in the country. We have observed that funding and support from the government combined with venues that allow the flow and sharing of knowledge enabled researchers to advance the growth of the field. The lack of available resources provided researchers problems to work on and for innovations to surface. Through various means, we noted that researchers are able to be constantly updated on recent trends. Most of the works we presented in this paper focused only on text and it highlights that there are still room for speech to speech translation.

Acknowledgement

This work is supported in part by the Philippine Commission on Higher Education through the Philippine-California Advanced Research Institutes Project (no. IIID-2015-07).

References

Alcantara,D.L., Hong, B.A., Perez, A., Tan, L. and Tan, M.W. (2006). Rule Extraction Applied in Language Translation. In *Proceedings of the 3rd Natural Language Processing Research Symposium*, pages 19–22, Manila, Philippines.

Allman, T., Beale, S. and Denton, R. (2014). Toward an Optimal Multilingual Natural Language Generator: Deep Source Analysis and Shallow Target Analysis. *Philippine Computing Journal*, 9(1): 55–63.

Allman, T. (2015). Linguist's Assistant: Gleaning a Tagalog Lexicon and Grammar from a Small, Lightly Annotated Corpus. In *Proceedings of the 11th Natural Language Processing Research Symposium*, page 1, Manila, Philippines.

Ananayo, J., Cayaos, J.D. and Rosal, F.G. (2011). Translation Algorithm: English to Kankanaey. In *Proceedings of the 8th Natural Language Processing Research Symposium*, pages 11–16, Manila, Philippines.

Ang, J., Chan, M.R., Genato, J.P., Uy, J. and Ilao, J. (2015). Development of a Filipino-to-English Bidirectional Statistical Machine Translation System that dynamically updates via user feedback. In *Proceedings of the 12th International Workshop on Spoken Language Translation*, Da Nang, Vietnam.

Bautista, J., Bayla, C., Fianza, K., Mamis, D., Tangangco, J., Yango, J. and Miguel, D. (2019). Bi-directional Ilocano-English Language Translator Using Customized Moses Statistical Machine Translation System (SMTS). In *Proceedings of the 11th Natural Language Processing Research Symposium*, pages 18–25, Manila, Philippines.

Borra, A. (1999). A Transfer-Based Engine for an English to Filipino Machine Translation Software. MS Thesis, University of the Philippines Los Baños.

Borra, A. Chan, E.A., Lim, C.I., Tan, R.B. and Tong, M.C. (2007). LFG-Based Machine Translation Engine for English and Filipino. In *Proceedings of the 4th Natural Language Processing Research Symposium*, pages 36–42, Manila, Philippines.

Cada, D.R., Chan, F.A., Chen, H.Z. and Tan, A.E. (2012). Bootstrapping a Tagalog LFG F-structure Bank. Undergraduate Thesis, De La Salle University.

Cubar, E. and Cubar, N. (1994). *Writing Filipino Grammar: Traditions and Trends*. New Day Publishers.

Dimalen, D.M., Dimalen, E., Pangandaman, M. and Wade, J. (2009). MELT: Towards Buidling an Indigenous MT System in Meanao to English Language. In *Proceedings of the 6th Natural Language Processing Research Symposium*, pages 34–37, Manila, Philippines.

Dimalen, D.M. and Roxas, R. (2007). AutoCor: A Query Based Automatic Acquisition of Corpora of Closely-related Languages. In *Proceedings of the 21st Pacific Asia Conference on Language, Information and Computation*, pages 146–154, Seoul, South Korea.

Fernandez, J.D., Jadie, J., Lim, C.K., Zuniega, J. and Llovido, J. (2018). Bi-directional Bikol-English Statistical Machine Translator. Presented at the *14th National Natural Language Processing Research Symposium Pre-Conference Activity: Student Research Workshop*, Legazpi, Philippines.

Frank, A., King, T.H., Kuhn, J. and Maxwell, J. (1998). Optimality Theory style constraint ranking in large-scale LFG grammars. In *Proceedings of the 3rd LFG Conference*, Brisbane, Australia.

Ilao, J., Roxas, R., Sison-Buban, R., Cheng, C., See, S. and Regalado, R.V. (2016). Philippine Component of the ASEAN Machine Translation Project. Paper presented at the *12th Natural Language Processing Research Symposium*, Dumaguete, Philippines.

Kroeger, P. (1993). *Phrase Structure and Grammatical Relations in Tagalog*. CSLI Publications.

Lat, J.O., Ng, S.T., Sze, K., Yu, G.D. and Lim, N.R. (2006). Lexicon Acquisition for the English and Filipino Language. In *Proceedings of the 3rd Natural Language Processing Research Symposium*, pages 49–54, Manila, Philippines.

Lazaro, A.N., Oco, N. and Roxas, R.E. (2017). Developing a Bidirectional Ilocano-English Translator for the Travel Domain: Using Domain Adaptation Techniques on Religious Parallel Corpora. Presented at the *11th International Conference of the Asian Association for Lexicography*, Guangzhou, China.

Macabante, D.G., Tambanillo, J.C. Dela Cruz, A. Ellema, N., Octaviano, M. Rodriguez, R. and Roxas, R.E. (2017). Bi-directional English-Hiligaynon statistical machine translation. In *Proceedings of TENCON 2017 - 2017 IEEE Region 10 Conference*, pages 2852–2853, Penang, Malaysia.

Miguel, D. and Dy, M.C. (2008). ANGLOCANO: an Ilocano to English Machine Translation System. In *Proceedings of the 5th Natural Language Processing Research Symposium*, pages 85–92, Manila, Philippines.

Nocon, N., Oco, N., Ilao, J. and Roxas, R E. (2014). Philippine Component of the Network-based ASEAN Language Translation Public Service. In *Proceedings of the 7th International Conference on Humanoid, Nanotechnology, Information Technology, Communication and Control, Environment, and Management*, Puerto Princesa City, Philippines.

Oco, N. and Borra, A. (2011). A Grammar Checker for Tagalog using LanguageTool. In *Proceedings of the 9th Workshop on Asian Language Resource Collocated with IJCNLP 2011*, pages 2–9, Chiang Mai, Thailand.

Oco, N., Syliongka, L.R., Allman, T. and Roxas, R.E. (2016). Resources for Philippine Languages: Collection, Annotation, and Modeling. In *Proceedings of the 30th Pacific Asia Conference on Language, Information, and Computation*, pages 433–438, Seoul, South Korea.

Octaviano, M., Dela Cruz, A., Oco, N. and Roxas, R.E. (2018). Cross-Lingual Topic Discovery. Presented at the *18th Philippine Computing Science Congress*, Cagayan de Oro, Philippines.

Raga, R. (2016). Reflections on the Awareness and Progress of Natural Language Processing (NLP) Research in the Philippines. *Philippine Computing Journal*, 11(1):1–9.

Ramos, T. (1971). *Makabagong Balarila ng Pilipino*. Rex Book Store.

Ramos, T. and Cena, R. (1990). *Modern Tagalog: Grammatical Explanations and Exercises for Non-native Speakers*. University of Hawaii Press.

Roxas, R.E., Sanchez, W. and Buenaventura, M. (1999). Machine Translation from English to Filipino: Second Phase. Report submitted to the Department of Science and Technology – Philippine Council for Advanced Science and Technology Research and Development.

Roxas, R.E. (2006). A Hybrid English-Filipino Machine Translation System. In *Proceedings of the 3rd Natural Language Processing Research Symposium*, pages 1–4, Manila, Philippines.

Roxas, R.E., Borra, A., Cheng, C., Lim, N.R., Ong, E.C. and Tan, M.W. (2008). Building language resources for a Multi-Engine English-Filipino machine translation system. *Language Resources and Evaluation*, 42:183–195.

Schachter, P. and Otanes, F. (1972). *Tagalog Reference Grammar*. University of California Press.

Tabaranza, Z.L., Bureros, L. and Roxas, R. (2016). English-Cebuano Parallel Language Resource for Statistical Machine Translation System. In *Proceedings of the 11th International Symposium on Natural Language Processing*, Ayutthaya, Thailand.

Tacorda, A.J., Ignacio, M.J., Oco, N. and Roxas, R.E. (2017). Controlling Byte Pair Encoding for Neural Machine Translation. In *Proceedings of the 21st International Conference on Asian Language Processing*, Singapore, Singapore.

Yara, J. (2007). A Tagalog-to-Cebuano Affix-Transfer-Based Machine Translator. In *Proceedings of the 4th Natural Language Processing Research Symposium*, pages 32–35, Manila, Philippines.

Semi-Supervised Neural Machine Translation with Language Models

Ivan Skorokhodov iskorokhodov@gmail.com

Anton Rykachevskiy anton.rykachevskiy@skolkovotech.ru
Skolkovo Intsitute of Science and Technology, Moscow, Russia

Dmitry Emelyanenko dimdi-y@ya.ru
National Research University Higher School of Economics, Moscow, Russia

Sergey Slotin me@sereja.me
Moscow Institute of Physics and Technology, Dolgoprudnyy, Russia

Anton Ponkratov anton.ponkratov@skolkovotech.ru
Skolkovo Intsitute of Science and Technology, Moscow, Russia

Abstract

Training neural machine translation models is notoriously slow and requires abundant parallel corpora and computational power. In this work we propose an approach of transferring knowledge from separately trained language models to translation systems, also we investigate several techniques to improve translation quality when there is a lack of parallel data and computational resources. Our method is based on fusion between translation system and language model, and initialization of translation system with weights from pretrained language models. We show that this technique gives +2.2 BLEU score on En–Fr pair of `WMT europarl-7` dataset and allows us to reach 20.7 BLEU on 20k parallel sentences in less than 8 hours of training on a single NVIDIA GeForce GTX 1080 Ti. We specifically note, that for this advance we use nothing but monolingual corpora for source and target languages. Significant part of presented results was obtained during DeepHack.Babel hackathon on low-resource machine translation organized by iPavlov Lab.

1 Introduction

Neural Machine Translation (NMT) is now a state-of-the-art approach for building translation systems. The reason behind this is both the invention of new techniques (Bahdanau et al., 2014) and availability of massive amounts of training data. Despite of abundance of parallel datasets for some popular language pairs we still lack such learning opportunities for many others. That's why there is a growing interest in techniques which allow us to train translation systems in semi-supervised or completely unsupervised fashion.

Several notable approaches (Conneau et al., 2017; Artetxe et al., 2017; Lample et al., 2017) in this direction were provided in recent years, but supervised techniques still highly outperform unsupervised ones. In our work we investigate a semi-supervised approach of combining translation model with language models in two ways. First, we propose an approach of initializing a translation model with language models and show how it can be used to advance learning of the whole translation system. Second, we revise the technique of shallow fusion by Gülçehre et al. (2015) by using two separate gates to combine predictions of the translation model with predictions of the language model. Using both of these techniques we were able to obtain +2.2 BLEU on `WMT europarl-7` data for En–Fr pair in comparison to the strong baseline model.

Most of the current work was preformed during the DeepHack.Babel hackathon[1] on unsupervised machine translation, organized by iPavlov Lab[2]. Participants were given the task to build semi-supervised translation system. Dataset consisted of 1M monolingual sentences for each of two languages (source and target) and 50k parallel sentences. The hackathon had an unusual format: instead of Kaggle-like submissions, where participants are given both training and test data and are asked to send predictions for the test set, we had to pack our models into Docker[3] containers and send it to the submission server, which did all the training and testing on its own side. The purpose of this was to prevent participants from deviating from the hackathon rules by using additional parallel datasets or incorporating some language-dependent techniques.

As the datasets used during the hackathon are private and not available for public use, we rerun all our experiments on a dataset, specially generated from WMT'14 En–Fr data (see section 4), and all the reported results are obtained from it. In such a way, we manage to build a system which learns to translate from English to French in less than 8 hours of training on NVIDIA GeForce GTX 1080 Ti by using only 20k parallel sentences and 300k monolingual corpora. Our system obtains 20.7 BLEU score, showing improvement of 2.2 BLEU in comparison to the strong baseline model, which does not use monolingual corpora.

2 Related work

Large amounts of monolingual corpora makes it very appealing to incorporate unsupervised methods into machine translation techniques, and in recent years this trend is becoming more and more prominent.

Cheng et al. (2016) and Sennrich et al. (2015) propose an approach of *backtranslation*, which is training two translation models: source→target and target→source, and then generating synthetic training dataset from monolingual corpora to improve the models. In such a way we incorporate the dual nature of the translation problem. Authors report significant improvement up to +3.7 BLEU on English→German pair on IWSLT'14 dataset (Sennrich et al., 2015).

Gülçehre et al. (2015) show how one can improve their translation model by shallow or deep fusion of separately trained language model. Let $p(\boldsymbol{y}_t = k|\boldsymbol{x}, \boldsymbol{y}_{<t})$ be a probability that t-th word of output sequence $\boldsymbol{y}$ is the k-th word of the vocabulary under some sequence-to-sequence model. Here $\boldsymbol{x}$ is the input sentence, $\boldsymbol{y}_{<t}$ are previous $t-1$ tokens. In shallow fusion we combine probabilities from target language model and translation model in the following way:

$$\log p(\boldsymbol{y}_t = k|\boldsymbol{x}, \boldsymbol{y}_{<t}) = \log p_{\text{trans}}(\boldsymbol{y}_t = k|\boldsymbol{x}, \boldsymbol{y}_{<t}) + \beta \log p_{\text{trg}}(\boldsymbol{y}_t = k|\boldsymbol{y}_{<t}),$$

where hyperparameter β denotes how much influence language model has for the prediction. In deep fusion authors just concatenate hidden states of the translation model and language model and fine-tune the whole thing, keeping parameters of the language model freeze.

Mikolov et al. (2013) used distributed representations of words to learn a linear mapping between vector spaces of languages and showed that this mapping can serve as a good dictionary between the languages. They pick 5k most frequent words from the source language $(\boldsymbol{x}_i)_{i=1}^{5000}$

[1]`http://babel.tilda.ws`

[2]`http://ipavlov.ai`

[3]`https://www.docker.com/`

and looked up their translations $(\boldsymbol{y}_i)_{i=1}^{5000}$ via Google Translate. Afterwards they used them to find a linear mapping W which minimizes $\sum_{i=1}^{5000} \parallel W\boldsymbol{x}_i - \boldsymbol{y}_i \parallel$. This linear mapping W was later utilized as the translation mapping to generate a dictionary between two vocabularies and proved to be rather accurate, giving almost 90% top-5 precision.

Lample et al. (2017) extended the approach of (Mikolov et al., 2013) and trained a Generative Adversarial Network (GAN) model to find this mapping without any supervised signal whatsoever. Generator was set to be this linear mapping, while discriminator should distinct between $\boldsymbol{y}$ and $\hat{\boldsymbol{y}} = W\boldsymbol{x}$. This approach worked out: learning random bijection was impossible because of linearity and learning a bad linear mapping was impossible, because many source words would be mapped to nowhere, which is heavily penalized by discriminator. Authors report 83.3% top-1 precision, which is a significant result for purely unsupervised approach.

Artetxe et al. (2017) built upon described methods to train translation model without any parallel corpora at all. They trained a shared encoder which should encode sentences into the language-agnostic representations and then two separate decoders to reconstruct them into the desired language. To make the encoding task non-trivial authors add noise to the input sentence: they randomly swap words, forcing encoder to learn internal structure of the sentence. They also use backtranslation procedure to make model learn to translate. This approach obtained 15.56 BLEU on Fr-En pair on WMT'14 dataset.

Artetxe et al. (2017) goes further and use adversarial loss to train their translation system. They build a single shared encoder and a single shared decoder, using both denoising autoencoder loss and adversarial loss. Corrupted version of the sentence is given to the encoder and its original form is reconstructed by the decoder. Discriminator takes encoder's outputs and tries to guess which language was given to the encoder. Backtranslation is also used to teach model to translate. Such an approach shows striking performance, obtaining 32.8 BLEU on English-French pair of Multi30k-Task1 dataset.

Zoph et al. (2016) experimented with transferring different components of the translation model trained on a rich language pair (parent model) to a low-resource NMT system (child model). Such a pretraining proved to be a very strong prior for the child model parameters and improved performance by an average of 5.6 BLEU.

3 Proposed approach

Our method is built upon Transformer (Vaswani et al., 2017) architecture, which proved to be a fast and powerful machine translation model. In the original paper, Transformer was trained entirely on a parallel data. In our work we propose several improvements over it which allows us to exploit monolingual corpora and learn in semi-supervised fashion.

3.1 Transformer model

Transformer (Vaswani et al., 2017) has general encoder-decoder architecture, but unlike RNN-based models, it is purely attentional, i.e. it does not keep any internal hidden state, which is recurrently updated, and all computations are done with tokens representations. Transformer takes a sequence as an input, makes several self-attentional iterations to encode it and then several attentional iterations to decode it. Attention mechanism (scaled dot-product attention) in its general form is defined as:

$$\text{Attention}(Q, K, V) = \text{softmax}\Big(\frac{QK^\top}{\sqrt{d}}\Big)V,$$

where Q is some query matrix (individual queries are packed into a query matrix), K is the keys which are used to process the query, V are the values to be retrieved. Transformer uses multiple attention heads:

$$\text{MultiHead}(Q, K, V) = [\text{head}_1, ..., \text{head}_h]W^O,$$

where $\text{head}_i = \text{Attention}(QW_i^Q, KW_i^K, VW_i^V)$. For translation setup we usually set $Q = K = V = [z_1, ..., z_k]^\top$ where z_i is the i-th sequence element on the current iteration. Scaling factor $\sqrt{d}$ improves numerical stability and does not allow model to be pushed to regions with flat gradients.

Each time attentional layer is computed, we apply a ReLU non-linearity with residual connections.

As Transformer does not possess any recurrent state, it needs to know a position of each token some other way. For this purpose we add a positional embedding $\boldsymbol{p}_i$ to each token $\boldsymbol{z}_i$, which elements are computed as:

$$p_i[j] = \begin{cases} \sin\left(i/10000^{\frac{2j}{d}}\right), & j \text{ is even;} \\ \cos\left(i/10000^{\frac{2j}{d}}\right), & j \text{ is odd.} \end{cases}$$

3.2 Initializing transformer with language models

Originally, transformer is trained in a purely supervised fashion, which limits its use to problems with abundant parallel corpora. We mitigate this problem the following way.

We take two monolingual corpora for each language, source and target, separately train Transformer's encoder as a language model for the source language, its decoder — as a language model for the target language, and then fine-tune the whole thing on a parallel corpus to learn a translation task. In this way, our method can be seen as a transfer learning technique.

Language model (LM) is tasked to predict the next token given the sequence of previous ones. Let $p_{\text{src}}(\boldsymbol{x}_s = l|\boldsymbol{x}_{<s}; \boldsymbol{\theta}_{\text{src}}), p_{\text{trg}}(\boldsymbol{y}_t = k|\boldsymbol{y}_{<t}; \boldsymbol{\theta}_{\text{trg}})$ denote language models for source and target languages, $p_{\text{trans}}(\boldsymbol{y}_t|\boldsymbol{x}, \boldsymbol{y}_{<t}; \boldsymbol{\theta})$ denote our Transformer. Source LM is parametrized as Transformer's encoder but with additional linear output transformation to generate logits, target LM — as its decoder but without encoder's outputs attention weights. One can notice that a lot of weights between $\boldsymbol{\theta}$ and $\{\boldsymbol{\theta}_{\text{src}}, \boldsymbol{\theta}_{\text{trg}}\}$ can be shared: $\boldsymbol{\theta}$ does not need final output connection from hidden state to logits of the source LM which $\boldsymbol{\theta}_{\text{src}}$ disposes and additionally it needs attention weights for encoder outputs from the decoder which $\boldsymbol{\theta}_{\text{trg}}$ lacks. All other weights can be transferred from language models to the translation model right away. In such a way we transfer knowledge, extracted by language models from large monolingual corpora, to our translation system. Transformer architecture with proposed initialization approach is represented on figure .

3.3 Gated shallow fusion

We further improve our model by incorporating language knowledge in the process of generating output sequence. In such a way we follow a strategy of shallow fusion proposed by Gülçehre et al. (2015), but instead of adding hyperparameter β we use *gated* shallow fusion. Let $\log p_{\text{trans}}(\boldsymbol{y}_t = k|\boldsymbol{x}, \boldsymbol{y}_{<t}), \log p_{\text{trg}}(\boldsymbol{y}_t = k|\boldsymbol{y}_{<t})$ denote logits for t-th output token produced by translation transformer and LM of the target language respectively. We generate final predictions $\log p(\boldsymbol{y}_t = k|\boldsymbol{x}, \boldsymbol{y}_{<t})$ in the following manner:

$$\log p(\boldsymbol{y}_t = k|\boldsymbol{x}, \boldsymbol{y}_{<t}) = \sigma_{\text{trans}}^{(t)} \cdot \log p_{\text{trans}}(\boldsymbol{y}_t = k|\boldsymbol{x}, \boldsymbol{y}_{<t}) + \sigma_{\text{lm}}^{(t)} \cdot \log p_{\text{trg}}(\boldsymbol{y}_t = k|\boldsymbol{y}_{<t}),$$

where $\sigma_{\text{trans}}^{(t)}, \sigma_{\text{lm}}^{(t)} \in (0, 1)$ are gates which let the overall system choose between two models. Both gates are produced by a feed-forward network with one hidden layer and two output neurones:

$$[\sigma_{\text{trans}}^{(t)}, \sigma_{\text{lm}}^{(t)}]^\top = \text{FFN}(\boldsymbol{s}_{\text{trans}}^{(t)})$$

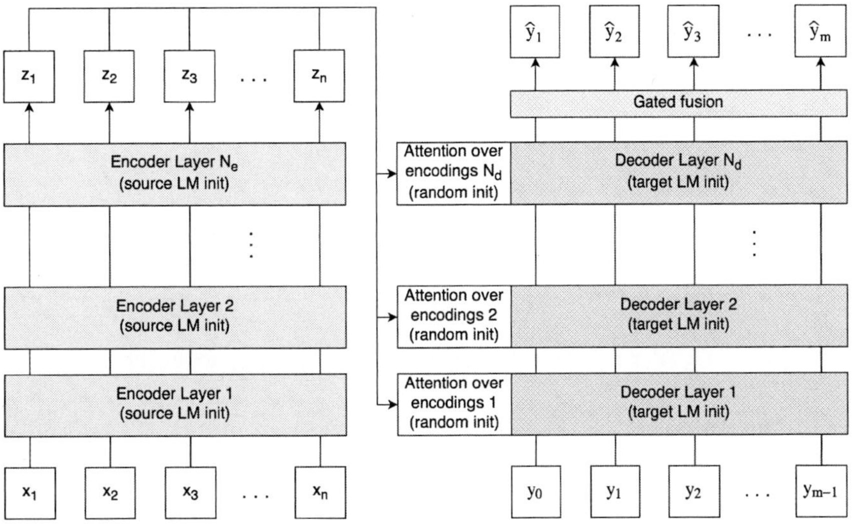

Figure 1: Proposed Transformer architecture. We color components whose weights are initialized with source LM weights in green, and with target LM — in blue.

We use two separate gates, σ_{trans} and σ_{lm}, instead of using a single one and gating with σ and $(1 - \sigma)$ because it gives more accurate calibration between the language model and translation model.

During training in this setup we freeze language model weights and translation model should learn when and how much it should trust language model.

4 Setup

In this section we describe datasets we used for testing our models, preprocessing steps and model parameters. Results are presented in the next section.

4.1 Datasets

To introduce repeatable results, we reproduced all experiments on famous `WMT europarl-v7` for En–Fr pair. This corpus consists of almost 2M parallel sentences, so we were able to extract parallel data, test set, and monolingual corpora for language models from it. Important thing here is that we choose monolingual corporas from different parts of original parallel corpora, so they do not contain similar information. Also we made experiments with different sizes of parallel corpora. We name datasets according to the size of the parallel corpus and language pair, see table 1. At the same time we used private dataset from DeepHack hackathon, which consists of descriptions of hotels in English and Russian as parallel corporas and comments about hotels as monolingual ones. The size of the parallel corpora for this set was originally 50k, and monolingual corporas were 1M each, but we reduced them to be the same size as En–Fr datasets.

We use validation set to prevent overfitting and reduce training time. Training process stops when the BLEU score on validation set does not improve for five epochs. The model with best validation BLEU at that moment is a final one. We report final result on 5k parallel sentences used as test set.

Dataset	Corpus	En	Fr
En–Fr-20k	Parallel train	0 - 20k	0 - 20k
	Parallel validation	47.5 - 48.5k	47.5 - 48.5k
	Parallel test	50 - 55k	50 - 55k
	Monolingual En	200 - 500k	-
	Monolingual Fr	-	1M - 1.3M
Fr-10k	Parallel train	0 - 10k	0 - 10k
	Parallel validation	47.5 - 48.5k	47.5 - 48.5k
	Parallel test	50 - 55k	50 - 55k
	Monolingual En	200 - 500k	-
	Monolingual Fr	-	1M - 1.3M

Table 1: Data splits from original `europarl-7` for En–Fr pair

4.2 Preprocessing

We use the following preprocessing procedure.

1. First, we tokenize all data with standard NLTK[4] package for python.
2. Second, we apply byte-pair encoding (Sennrich et al., 2015) to reduce the size of the dictionary. This step is done using Subword-NMT[5] library. For En–Fr pair we use joint vocabulary of size 32k. And for En-Ru we use separate vocabularies 4k each. Vocabularies are fixed for all En–Fr datasets and for all En-Ru datasets.

4.3 Default model

For translation model we follow general transformer architecture (Vaswani et al., 2017), but as we were highly constrained by time and computational resources during the hackathon (we had 8 hours on NVIDIA GeForce GTX 1080 Ti for preprocessing, training and inference), we had to reduce several hyper-parameters values.

Model we used had the following parameters for all experiments: All embeddings had size $d = 512$, hidden layer of FFN, applied to embeddings in between attentional layers, had 2048 neurons. We used 4 attentional heads and 4 attentional layers. Our dropout rates were chosen to be 0.1 for attention, ReLU and residual connections. As an optimizer we used Adam optimizer with initial learning rate being equal $1e-4$ and $\beta_2 = 0.98$. Weights are randomly initialized with normal distribution with mean 0 and standard deviation being equal $1/\sqrt{d}$.

5 Results

In this section we evaluate all variations of model on several datasets, to see how our models profits from fusion and initialization with language models.

5.1 20k experiments[6]

We start from evaluating four main models on En–Fr-20k and En-Ru-20k datasets. The training progress for En–Fr pair is shown on Fig. 2. The final results for both pairs on a test set are listed in table 2. We can notice, that models with initialization perform reasonably better than models without it. Also we see that initialization is essential if we use fusion. All training process for 20k data fits in 5 hours on GTX 1080 Ti, and a huge part of this time is used by validation after each epoch.

[4]http://www.nltk.org

[5]https://github.com/rsennrich/subword-nmt

[6]20k parallel train sentences, 1k parallel validation sentences, 300k monolingual corporas

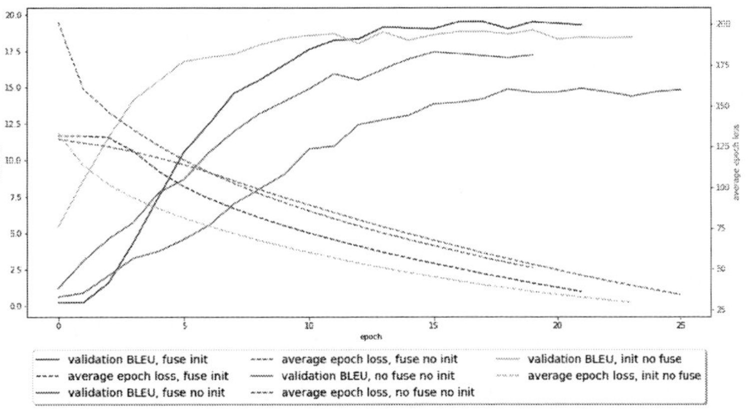

Figure 2: Training process for En–Fr-20k dataset

Model	BLEU En–Fr	BLEU En-Ru
Transformer	18.5	26.3
Transformer with LM initialization	19.7	27.7
Transformer without LM initialization, with fusion	16.1	26.0
Transformer with LM initialization and fusion	20.7	27.2

Table 2: Results on 20k datasets

5.2 10k experiments

During this series of experiments we see again that proposed approach improves BLEU score. Also it is worth to mention that for fused model this initialization is essential to achieve any reasonable score. Finally it is important to notice, that due to extremely small parallel corpora models tend to do a lot of factual mistakes in translations, which is shown well by BLEU score.

Model	BLEU En–Fr	BLEU En-Ru
Transformer	13.6	21.8
Transformer with LM initialization	16.1	23.0
Transformer without LM initialization, with fusion	<5	21.8
Transformer with LM initialization and fusion	15.9	22.4

Table 3: Results on 10k datasets

6 Discussion and Conclusion

In this work we presented an approach of initializing translation model with language models and a new technique for shallow fusion of LM into translation system. These approaches allow to improve existing NMT in the situations when there is a lack of parallel data by only using monolingual corpora. We experimentally showed an improvement up to +2.5 BLEU for the Transformer model on one of the setups. However we must notice that human review of translations for En-Ru pair where our model outperformed standard transformer by 1.4 BLEU, does not show any significant advantage of our approach. All of the proposed models perform quite well on short sentences and provide almost the same translations but on the sentences longer than 15 words, translations become notably different and with different mistakes. Also, we see that the performance of our version of fusion is not always good so this approach is yet to be analyzed.

Acknowledgment

We thank iPavlov laboratory for organizing DeepHack.Babel hackathon and providing us data and computational resources to do the work.

References

Artetxe, M., Labaka, G., Agirre, E., and Cho, K. (2017). Unsupervised neural machine translation. *Computing Research Repository*, abs/1710.11041.

Bahdanau, D., Cho, K., and Bengio, Y. (2014). Neural machine translation by jointly learning to align and translate. *Computing Research Repository*, abs/1409.0473.

Cheng, Y., Xu, W., He, Z., He, W., Wu, H., Sun, M., and Liu, Y. (2016). Semi-supervised learning for neural machine translation. *Computing Research Repository*, abs/1606.04596.

Conneau, A., Lample, G., Ranzato, M., Denoyer, L., and Jégou, H. (2017). Word translation without parallel data. *Computing Research Repository*, abs/1710.04087.

Gülçehre, Ç., Firat, O., Xu, K., Cho, K., Barrault, L., Lin, H., Bougares, F., Schwenk, H., and Bengio, Y. (2015). On using monolingual corpora in neural machine translation. *Computing Research Repository*, abs/1503.03535.

Lample, G., Denoyer, L., and Ranzato, M. (2017). Unsupervised machine translation using monolingual corpora only. *Computing Research Repository*, abs/1711.00043.

Mikolov, T., Le, Q. V., and Sutskever, I. (2013). Exploiting similarities among languages for machine translation. *Computing Research Repository*, abs/1309.4168.

Sennrich, R., Haddow, B., and Birch, A. (2015). Improving neural machine translation models with monolingual data. *Computing Research Repository*, abs/1511.06709.

Vaswani, A., Shazeer, N., Parmar, N., Uszkoreit, J., Jones, L., Gomez, A. N., Kaiser, L., and Polosukhin, I. (2017). Attention is all you need. *Computing Research Repository*, abs/1706.03762.

Zoph, B., Yuret, D., May, J., and Knight, K. (2016). Transfer learning for low-resource neural machine translation. *CoRR*, abs/1604.02201.

System description of Supervised and Unsupervised Neural Machine Translation approaches from "NL Processing" team at DeepHack.Babel task

Ilya Gusev ilya.gusev@phystech.edu
MIPT, Dolgoprudny, Moscow Region, 141701, Russian Federation
Artem Oboturov oboturov@gmail.com

Abstract

A comparison [1] of supervised and unsupervised Neural Machine Translation (NMT) models was done for the corpora provided by the DeepHack.Babel competition. It is shown that for even small parallel corpus, fully supervised NMT gives better results than fully unsupervised for the case of constrained domain of the corpus. We have also implemented a fully unsupervised and a semi-supervised NMT models which have not given positive results compared to fully supervised models. A blind set-up is described where participants know at no point what language pair is used for translation, so no extra data could be integrated in pre-submission phase or during training. Finally, future competition organizers should find ways to protect their competition set-ups against various attacks in order to prevent from revealing of language pairs. We have reported two possible types of attacks on the blind set-up.

1 Competition Set-up

The work presented here is motivated by the following observation: an industrial Neural Machine Translation (NMT) system is usually built on a huge parallel corpora and trained for days or even weeks. A "raw" NMT model is then tuned by additional training on client-specific data and by augmentation with some domain-specific information. What if it is not as important to have such a heavy and difficult-to-train model? Instead, why not just use a simple bootstart model based only on the client's data with a subsequent augmentation done using unsupervised learning, which would use any available non-parallel corpora? If such approach would produce results comparable to models trained on large parallel corpora, one could significantly reduce costs of preparing parallel corpora and instead focus on better unsupervised models which work with non-parallel corpora (which are much easier and cheaper to produce). It might also help for the case of low resource languages when no large parallel corpora exist. This paper attempts to answer these questions.

We present the results obtained by the "NL Processing" team in the DeepHack.Babel hackathon [2] on semi-supervised machine translation. Organizers of the competition created a blind set-up - a case in which the source and target languages are not known at any stage of

[1]Images used to train models are publicly available at https://github.com/aoboturov/loresmt-nlprocessing

[2]The leaderboard: http://contest.deephack.me/c/babel/leaderboard

the competition and the machine translation system should be trained with no specific tuning to the language pair. Language pairs were trained and scored independently, so no one sought to build a universal model. Training and translation were performed by the scoring system. Participants have no insight into the process and could only observe the final score for a submission and/or the failure status. For each language pair participants can submit multiple entries and, based on the scores, adapt their models. Submissions were scored in BLEU-4 (Papineni et al., 2002). The fact that the language pair was not known should have prevented participants from any specific tuning and pre-training of their submitted models; for each submitted model, it had a strict time limit for training and inference (8 hours in total for both stages) and a computational budget constrained by a single dedicated GPU. The participants' models were not allowed to access the internet or any external resources in the training and the evaluation process.

For each language pair the following datasets [3] were available:

- each language of a pair has one monolingual corpora, `1M` sentences;
- a small parallel corpus, `50K` sentence pairs;
- an input corpus to be translated from source to target language, `6K` sentences.

There were 3 language pairs used during the competition: `En-Ru` for test, `Lv-En` for qualification and `En-Ko` for final scoring. Data for training and test are not available publicly and organizers would not release them. Therefore we could only provide a summary [4]: Table 1 describes statistics for the corpora.

Pair	Source Tokens	Source Words	Target Tokens	Target Words
En-Ru	14M	165519	19M	345444
Lv-En	21M	502858	24M	341012
En-Ko	14M	157649	7M	530124

Table 1: Descriptive statistics for the corpora.

The machine translation system could be built as a fully supervised one, though the parallel corpus is small (`50K`); as an unsupervised one, using the two monolingual corpora; and as a semi-supervised one. Given the problem at hand, a simple fully supervised NMT baseline was implemented which was then compared against the Unsupervised Machine Translation Using Monolingual Corpora Only (UNMT) model which was trained both in fully unsupervised and semi-supervised modes.

To prepare for the DeepHack.Babel hackathon we looked into recent supervised NMT systems [5] including: Google's seq2seq (Britz et al., 2017), FAIR Sequence-to-Sequence Toolkit (Gehring et al., 2017), Marian-NMT (Junczys-Dowmunt et al., 2016a) and Sockeye (Hieber et al., 2017). For the competition, however, we focused on the theme of the hackathon, which was on unsupervised and semi-supervised models under the conditions of the blind set-up. The literature review indicated, that the blind set-up itself is novel: (Och et al., 2004), (Tillmann, 2004) and others call their experiments blind with respect to the hold-out set for the final scoring, but we were not able to find an experiment, which was blinded with respect to the language pair.

[3] Contest overview: `http://contest.deephack.me/c/babel/overview`

[4] Samples from the parallel corpora are provided online `https://github.com/aoboturov/loresmt-nlprocessing#the-corpora-extracts`

[5] One could find them on-line: `https://github.com/aoboturov/aoboturov-deephack-babel-qualification`

In Section 2 we outline the baseline that was used to benchmark the UNMT in the blind set-up. In Section 3 we discuss our experiments with the UNMT model for the blind set-up. Finally, in Section 4 we investigate whether prior knowledge of a language pair gives an advantage for the unsupervised NMT approach.

2 Baseline

A supervised NMT model [6] was chosen for the baseline. The model was implemented in OpenNMT (Klein et al., 2017) and had the following Encoder-Decoder architecture:

- the encoder is 3 LSTM layers with a dropout based on 300 dimensional word embeddings for the source language,
- the decoder is stacked LSTM layers with a dropout and a global attention (Luong et al., 2015) based on 300 dimensional word embeddings for the target language.

For each language pair a model was trained only on a `50K` parallel corpus with a `5%` validation set. Data were lowercased and tokenized with Moses (Koehn et al., 2007). Training on an NVIDIA Titan XP GPU usually lasted for 20 to 30 minutes, the results of which are provided in Table 2. Additionally, embeddings were trained with Fasttext (Bojanowski et al., 2017). We have a number of different combinations of LSTM depths and cell-sizes, but we did not search for optimal hyper parameters for the supervised baseline. We have realized that, even without optimal hyperparameters, the baseline beats the UNMT score by an order of magnitude.

On the `Lv-En` language pair, the model performance was mediocre. This could be explained by the fact that `En-Ru` and `En-Ko` were topic-restricted corpora. In particular, both were related to tourism only. On the other hand, the `Lv-En` corpus was extracted from a news feed which had no topic constraints.

3 Unsupervised Neural Machine Translation

The competition included not only parallel corpus for each language pair, but also `1M` monolingual corpus for each language. One way to leverage this data is to use unsupervised NMT model described in Lample et al. (2017). The code for this model is not available, so we built our own implementation [7] based on the PyTorch (Paszke et al., 2017) framework. One can train this model on monolingual corpora using a predefined initial model, which we refer to in this paper as the zero model. The goal of the competition was to find unsupervised and semi-supervised Machine Translation (MT) methods applicable in practice. A fully unsupervised case is covered in Section 3.1, while a semi-supervised approach is described in Section 3.2.

The UNMT [8] would train iteratively using adversarial training (Goodfellow, 2016) with a discriminator [9] presented in Figure 1. In both the semi-supervised and unsupervised cases we ran an unsupervised training epoch which starts from a batch of sentences translated by a model from a previous iteration of unsupervised training (or zero model if it is the first iteration) followed by a noising layer and a pass through the model that has been trained on the current iteration. The preprocessing was done with Moses (Koehn et al., 2007): data were lowercased and tokenized (except for Korean). Figure 2 gives a graphical explanation of the training process.

[6] For a full description of the Encoder-Decoder architecture see `https://github.com/aoboturov/loresmt-nlprocessing#supervised-model-description`.

[7] Implementation of the UNMT: `https://github.com/IlyaGusev/UNMT`

[8] The UNMT model used for translation is described in `https://github.com/aoboturov/loresmt-nlprocessing#unmt-model-description`

[9] The Discriminator description is available online `https://github.com/aoboturov/loresmt-nlprocessing#unmt-discriminator-description`

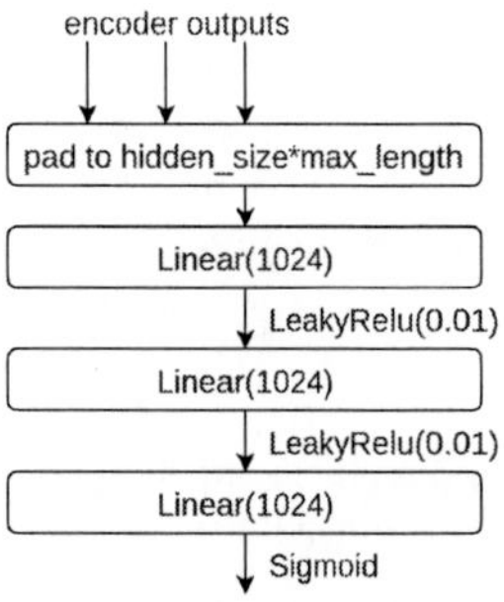

Figure 1: Adversarial training discriminator.

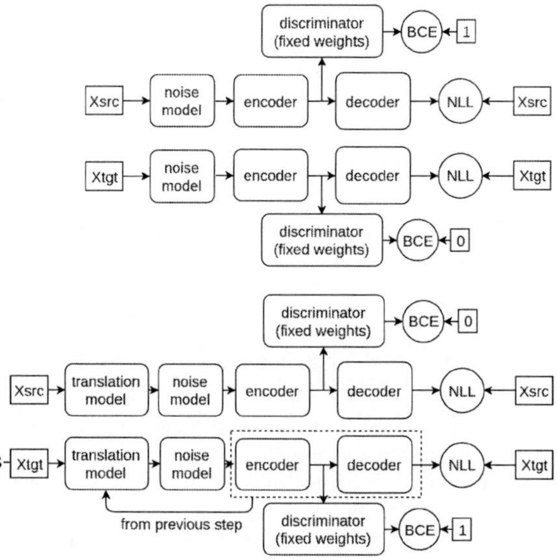

Figure 2: UNMT training process.

There are two types of zero models which we have used: dictionary translation, and a supervised model trained on a small corpora. The translation model has an RNN Encoder-Decoder architecture (Cho et al., 2014) with word embeddings and a global attention (Luong et al., 2015). Figure 3 depicts the encoder and Figure 4 presents the decoder.

3.1 UNMT with a dictionary translation zero model

The dictionary translation model is a translation process which uses a dictionary obtained with an unsupervised embedding (Conneau et al., 2017) (or otherwise an external dictionary could have been used if the language pair was known) to translate each sentence using dictionary translation.

To debug the zero model we first check the input to output copy which is reported in Table 2 as the `In to Out Copy` result. Normally, we would expect an improvement over the `In to Out Copy`, because it is closely related to dictionary translation: words which are not in the dictionary would be copied over from source to target sentences. BLEU scores on language pairs were below 0.01 `BLEU`.

3.2 UNMT with a fully supervised zero model

The fully supervised model was trained in the same way as the baseline. Although the model itself was the Encoder-Decoder from UNMT and not the one from the baseline. The zero model gives a 0.08 `BLUE`, UNMT after adversarial training lasting a day gave results well below 0.01 `BLEU`.

4 Prior Language Pair Information

In this section we describe how the blind set-up can be hacked to improve our results, given that the competition is structured so that the participants do not know the language-pairs being used, and it would be difficult to determine these language pairs within the scope of the competition. The hackathon could have had any pair-combination of 42 languages supported

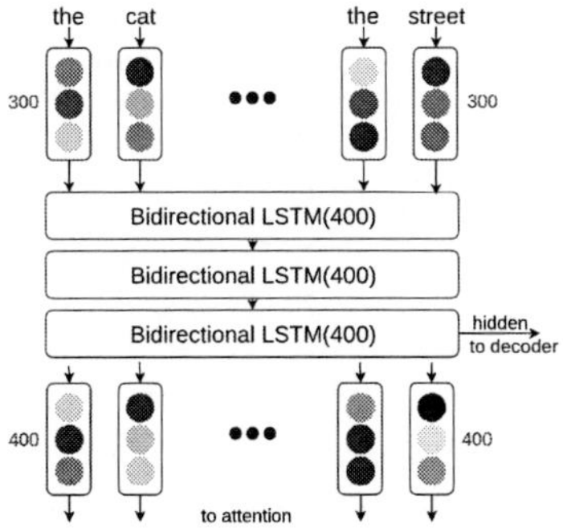

Figure 3: UNMT encoder.

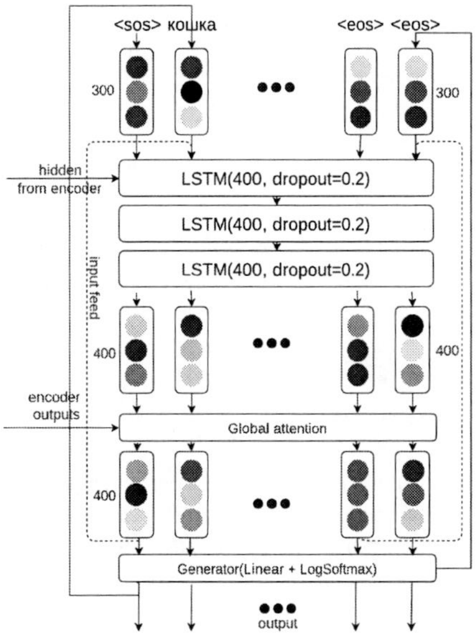

Figure 4: UNMT decoder.

by Booking.com, so the total number of models, if trained unidirectionally, would have been over 1500. Given that even for our simplest baseline model an individual NMT model is at least 300 megabytes, we would have had to train individual unidirectional models, likely for over several days, on some external parallel data, which we did not have for all language pairs, and to package around half of a terabyte of data inside a docker container, which is technologically unrealistic. We could have followed Google's NMT approach (Johnson et al., 2017) or any other MT approach, which have intermediate neural representation, to reduce the total number of models to just one, it should still have to be trained on external parallel corpora, even if they all would be just English to any other of the 41 languages. To reduce the combinatorial complexity of the problem, one could potentially identify the language pair and then just train a single unidirectional model. The competition testing system prevented the access to any external resources and remote calls during training and inference phases. The sheer size of model representations, the total training time, amount and diversity of training data and technical constraints would make pre-training a non-viable option. The only information available to participants was the BLEU score and the failure or success status for the submission. With these information, however, one could devise at least two attacks to identify the language pair and then using this prior knowledge, use it to construct a better translation algorithm.

In Table 2 we reported the best BLEU scores available within the conference submissions for each of the pairs trained on common corpora. On the one hand, we could see that a margin of improvement is just a couple of BLEU points for `En-Ru` and `En-Ko` pairs. On the other hand, `Lv-En` has a very poor result and we would expect that both unsupervised learning and prior knowledge may improve this score.

Below, we describe at least two ways how a language pair identification Side-Channel attack could be executed. The execution time attack is supposed to identify the language pair in a single submission, while the failure status attack would require multiple submissions. The number of submissions used to identify the language pair would matter when the total number

Model	En-Ru Score	Lv-En Score	En-Ko Score
Supervised, 10 Epochs	0.2892	0.0576	0.2542
In to Out Copy	0.0212	0.0208	0.0276
Unsupervised UNMT	-	0.0043	-
Semi-supervised UNMT	-	-	0.0018
Competitors Best	-	0.2334	0.3007
Literature Best, non-blind	0.2980	0.2290	0.2795

Table 2: Evaluation results for models in the blind set-up, measured in BLEU scores.

of submissions for the competition is limited.

4.1 Using Execution Time

There is a way to identify the language pair in one submission by using the side-channel attack technique. In this particular case, the side-channel would be the execution time of the translation algorithm whereby a language identification routine is run on each of the non-parallel corpora and both languages of the pair are detected. Given that the routine could identify N languages, all the pairs could be enumerated to define a mapping of natural numbers in the range $1 \ldots N * (N-1)$. Provided that a specific constant delay is used, one could divide the total execution time by the delay duration to obtain the index of the pair in the mapping.

4.2 Using Failure Status

The second way is a slower combinatorial way in which a failure status is used as an indicator of the language belonging to a subset of languages being tested. A set of all languages identifiable by the routine could be searched in log-time in a breadth-search fashion descending only into subsets where we have established an inclusion relationship.

5 Results and Conclusions

In Table 2, the first four models are the ones that we have produced for the competition, followed by the result reported by the winning team for each round. The last model is reported from literature reviews for the non-blind set-up. The best `Lv-En` and `En-Ru` are from the newstest2017 corpora in Bojar et al. (2017). `En-Ko` is reported from the work of Junczys-Dowmunt et al. (2016b), which uses COPPA corpus. The Literature Best models provide an indicative benchmark for what a MT system trained on a generic parallel corpus might score on a translation task when the language pair is known.

A generic fully unsupervised machine translation problem is hard. In some cases, one could obtain good machine translation models by having a small data set for a limited domain, e.g. for a case of traveling destinations or some other domain-specific translation. Although semi-supervised translation might improve the results, we have not observed that a fully supervised model used as the zero model for the UNMT made any translation improvement over a regular supervised model. For this particular UNMT architecture we report a negative result based on our experiments. Poor performance of the UNMT has to be investigated further, possibly by providing larger non-parallel corpora and changing UNMT model architecture.

References

Bojanowski, P., Grave, E., Joulin, A., and Mikolov, T. (2017). Enriching Word Vectors with Subword Information. *Transactions of the Association for Computational Linguistics*, 5:135–146.

Bojar, O., Chatterjee, R., Federmann, C., Graham, Y., Haddow, B., Huang, S., Huck, M., Koehn, P., Liu, Q., Logacheva, V., et al. (2017). Findings of the 2017 conference on machine translation (wmt17). In *Proceedings of the Second Conference on Machine Translation*, pages 169–214.

Britz, D., Goldie, A., Luong, M.-T., and Le, Q. (2017). Massive Exploration of Neural Machine Translation Architectures. In *Proceedings of the 2017 Conference on Empirical Methods in Natural Language Processing*, pages 1442–1451.

Cho, K., van Merrienboer, B., Gulcehre, C., Bahdanau, D., Bougares, F., Schwenk, H., and Bengio, Y. (2014). Learning Phrase Representations using RNN Encoder–Decoder for Statistical Machine Translation. In *Proceedings of the 2014 Conference on Empirical Methods in Natural Language Processing (EMNLP)*, pages 1724–1734.

Conneau, A., Lample, G., Ranzato, M., Denoyer, L., and Jégou, H. (2017). Word translation without parallel data. *arXiv preprint arXiv:1710.04087*.

Gehring, J., Auli, M., Grangier, D., Yarats, D., and Dauphin, Y. N. (2017). Convolutional Sequence to Sequence Learning. In *Proc. of ICML*.

Goodfellow, I. (2016). NIPS 2016 tutorial: Generative adversarial networks. *arXiv preprint arXiv:1701.00160*.

Hieber, F., Domhan, T., Denkowski, M., Vilar, D., Sokolov, A., Clifton, A., and Post, M. (2017). Sockeye: A Toolkit for Neural Machine Translation. *ArXiv e-prints*.

Johnson, M., Schuster, M., Le, Q. V., Krikun, M., Wu, Y., Chen, Z., Thorat, N., Viégas, F., Wattenberg, M., Corrado, G., et al. (2017). Google's Multilingual Neural Machine Translation System: Enabling Zero-Shot Translation. *Transactions of the Association for Computational Linguistics*, 5:339–351.

Junczys-Dowmunt, M., Dwojak, T., and Hoang, H. (2016a). Is Neural Machine Translation Ready for Deployment? A Case Study on 30 Translation Directions. In *Proceedings of the 9th International Workshop on Spoken Language Translation (IWSLT)*, Seattle, WA.

Junczys-Dowmunt, M., Pouliquen, B., and Mazenc, C. (2016b). COPPA V2. 0: Corpus Of Parallel Patent Applications Building Large Parallel Corpora with GNU Make. In *4 th Workshop on Challenges in the Management of Large Corpora Workshop Programme*, page 15.

Klein, G., Kim, Y., Deng, Y., Senellart, J., and Rush, A. M. (2017). OpenNMT: Open-Source Toolkit for Neural Machine Translation. In *Proc. ACL*.

Koehn, P., Hoang, H., Birch, A., Callison-Burch, C., Federico, M., Bertoldi, N., Cowan, B., Shen, W., Moran, C., Zens, R., et al. (2007). Moses: Open source toolkit for statistical machine translation. In *Proceedings of the 45th annual meeting of the ACL on interactive poster and demonstration sessions*, pages 177–180. Association for Computational Linguistics.

Lample, G., Denoyer, L., and Ranzato, M. (2017). Unsupervised machine translation using monolingual corpora only. *CoRR*, abs/1711.00043.

Luong, T., Pham, H., and Manning, C. D. (2015). Effective Approaches to Attention-based Neural Machine Translation. In *Proceedings of the 2015 Conference on Empirical Methods in Natural Language Processing*, pages 1412–1421.

Och, F. J., Gildea, D., Khudanpur, S., Sarkar, A., Yamada, K., Fraser, A., Kumar, S., Shen, L., Smith, D., Eng, K., et al. (2004). A smorgasbord of features for statistical machine translation. In *Proceedings of the Human Language Technology Conference of the North American Chapter of the Association for Computational Linguistics: HLT-NAACL 2004*.

Papineni, K., Roukos, S., Ward, T., and Zhu, W.-J. (2002). BLEU: a method for automatic evaluation of machine translation. In *Proceedings of the 40th annual meeting on association for computational linguistics*, pages 311–318. Association for Computational Linguistics.

Paszke, A., Gross, S., Chintala, S., Chanan, G., Yang, E., DeVito, Z., Lin, Z., Desmaison, A., Antiga, L., and Lerer, A. (2017). Automatic differentiation in PyTorch.

Tillmann, C. (2004). A unigram orientation model for statistical machine translation. In *Proceedings of HLT-NAACL 2004: Short Papers*, pages 101–104. Association for Computational Linguistics.

Apertium's Web Toolchain for Low-Resource Language Technology

Sushain Cherivirala sushain@skc.name
Independent Scholar, Apertium Community

Shardul Chiplunkar shardul.chiplunkar@gmail.com
Independent Scholar, Apertium Community

Jonathan North Washington jonathan.washington@swarthmore.edu
Linguistics Department, Swarthmore College, Swarthmore, PA 19081 USA

Kevin Brubeck Unhammer unhammer+apertium@mm.st
Trigram AS, Stavanger, Norway

Abstract

The Apertium web toolchain, consisting of a front end (Apertium HTML-Tools) and a back end (Apertium APy), is a free and open-source toolchain that supports a range of open-source technologies. The internationalised interface allows users to translate text, documents, and web pages, as well as morphologically analyse and generate text. Other features, including support for multi-step/pivot translation, dictionary-style lookup, spell-checking, and accepting user suggestions for translations, are nearing release.[1]

1 Introduction

Apertium APy[2] (API in Python) was begun in August 2013 as a drop-in replacement written in Python 3 for Apertium's previous query engine, ScaleMT[3], which was written in Java and was no longer maintained. Apertium HTML-Tools[4] was created later that year as a modern front end that interfaces with APy, replacing its less interactive predecessor. Both of these free and open-source (FOSS) applications constitute the Apertium web toolchain and have seen regular development and increased feature sets since their inception five years ago.

These tools were developed to make the FOSS language technology of Apertium (Forcada et al., 2011) available to a much wider audience than otherwise possible. Setting up the Apertium tools for use on a desktop operating system is a barrier to many who wish to use the tools, and their use on the command line can be cumbersome for tasks like translation, post-editing, and spell-checking.

[1] We appreciate support of this project by Google Code-In (2013–2017) and Google Summer of Code, and the time invested by GSoC students Kira Droganova (2016) and Monish Godhia (2017), as well as help from a number of contributors and translators.

[2] http://wiki.apertium.org/wiki/Apertium-apy

[3] http://wiki.apertium.org/wiki/ScaleMT

[4] http://wiki.apertium.org/wiki/Apertium-html-tools

Today, this infrastructure is deployed on the official Apertium website (apertium.org), the website for testing production and development Turkic-language tools (turkic.apertium.org), an "Apertium beta" site that makes available all of Apertium's language pairs regardless of development status (beta.apertium.org), and Giellatekno Apertium's translation site (jorgal.uit.no, maintained as a parallel branch). These sites allow anyone in the world with an Internet connection to make use of Apertium language technology.

APy is also used by Wikimedia Content Translation (Mistry et al., 2017), which facilitates the translation of content between Wikipedia articles in different languages, and the Sámi-language newspaper Ávvir[5], published in Norway, uses the spell- and grammar-checker back end for editing their publications. Similarly, Softcatalà, a non-profit association dedicated to fighting the marginalisation of the Catalan language, now employs APy as a translation service (Ivars-Ribes and Sánchez-Cartagena, 2011). Since the entire platform is FOSS, it is easily deployed on new systems and modified for specific uses.

This paper presents an overview of the web toolchain's architecture (§2), describes its core functionality (§3) and advanced features (§4), discusses on-going work (§5), summarises usage figures (§6), and concludes with thoughts on future work (§7).

2 Overview

The toolchain consists of a JavaScript/HTML/CSS front end called HTML-Tools and a Python 3.3+ back end called APy. The applications are type checked by Flow[6] and MyPy[7], respectively. The front end can function with any back end that supports the same API as APy; although almost all deployed versions of HTML-Tools are dependent on APy, it would be straightforward to have HTML-Tools use a custom back end developed for specific low-resource languages.

The back end can also be used as a general API for other purposes. For example, the IRC bot begiak[8] uses it to provide real-time translations and APy statistics, and the CAT tool OmegaT[9] has a plugin using APy.

HTML-Tools supports translation (of multiple text formats) and morphological functions in a fully internationalised environment. Currently the majority of the interface is localised in 25 languages. Responsive design makes the interface fluid on both mobile and desktop devices.

The machine translation (MT) endpoint of the API is, as with the ScaleMT system, similar to the Google Translate API, so MT consumers may easily switch between or support both APIs. Other endpoints support other functions, such as morphological analysis and generation, and provide localisation data to clients.

[5]https://avvir.no/
[6]https://flow.org/
[7]http://mypy-lang.org/
[8]http://wiki.apertium.org/wiki/Begiak
[9]https://omegat.org/

3 Core Features

The core feature of the Apertium web toolchain is the machine translation interface in HTML-Tools (Figure 1), which allows the user to choose a source and target language to translate their source text. Users may also use the language detection functionality powered by CLD2[10]. By allowing immediate access to three recently used languages, the interface facilitates switching between multiple frequently used languages.

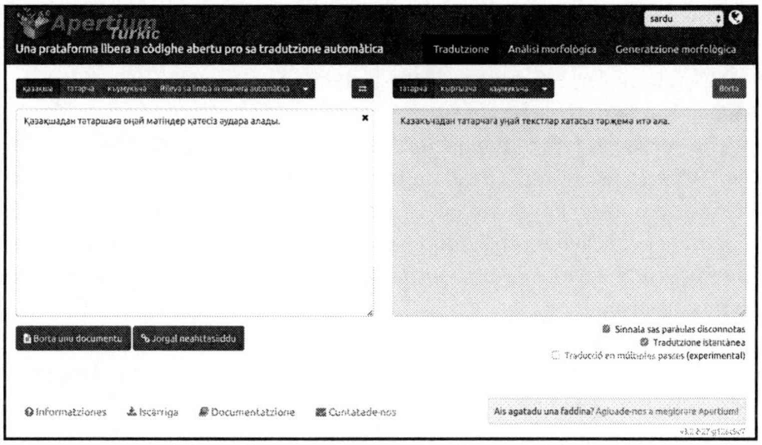

Figure 1: HTML-Tools' interface showing machine translation, and tabs for different modes. The screenshot also demonstrates localisation (Sardinian, with missing-string fallback to Northern Sámi) and a subtitle ("Turkic").

The toolchain offers a fully internationalised experience with the HTML-Tools' interface language defaulted to match the user's browser locale and manually controllable by a language selector. Both right-to-left and left-to-right scripts are supported. The interface's string localisations are located in JSON files, one for each language, that each contain some metadata and a simple key-value storage schema with support for basic templating. In addition to the interface's strings being localised, glossonym localisation is powered by APy where language names are fetched from a SQLite database. The database is populated from text files containing data from SIL International[11] and the Unicode Common Locale Data Repository[12] as well as manual curation[13]. Autoglossonyms (and following that, ISO 639-3 three-letter codes) are used as fallbacks when a language name is not localised in the interface's current language.

In contrast to many modern web applications, HTML-Tools eschews complex build dependencies and tools such as Webpack, requiring only GNU Make, `curl`,

[10]`https://github.com/CLD2Owners/cld2`
[11]`https://www.sil.org/`
[12]`http://cldr.unicode.org/`
[13]These scripts are bundled with APy.

and Python 3 in a standard POSIX environment to successfully build its static resources which can then be served by any web server. Performance optimisations such as resource compression are entirely optional and offline building and usage are supported.

APy is modeled after the ScaleMT infrastructure (Sánchez-Cartagena and Pérez-Ortiz, 2010). Every translation language pair (e.g., Catalan to Spanish) or monolingual analysis/generation pipeline corresponds to an Apertium `mode`, which is a Unix pipeline defined by the Apertium language data developers. Since pairs involve multiple executables running in serial accessing large binaries, it would be prohibitively slow to bootstrap a pair on each request, so pipelines are kept open between requests and flush data upon seeing a `NUL` character (which is added at the end of each request).[14]

The server is typically run in a single Python process using the Tornado library[15], which uses green threads to allow large numbers of asynchronous/non-blocking requests. Large requests are split into manageable sizes so they do not block the server even if other requests to the same `mode` come in. Like ScaleMT, APy allows opening several copies of the same `mode` in case of high traffic, and shutting down unused ones.

The process handling is general enough that it can make any Unix pipeline into a scalable, robust, non-blocking web service, as long as the pipeline can be made to flush output on seeing a certain input. The spell- and grammar-checking pipeline used by Ávvir (which does not use APy's built-in spelling backend) is one example of taking a "new" pipeline and using APy to turn it into a web service.

4 Advanced Features

The toolchain has first-class support for language variants, a feature particularly relevant to some low-resource languages. Within APy, all endpoints accept language codes with variants, e.g. `oci_aran` represents Aranese, a variety of Occitan. HTML-Tools provides special rendering to variants, as shown in Figure 2 where variants are always nested within their 'parent' languages to aid discoverability.

In HTML-Tools, all user inputs and selections are persisted in their browser's local storage unless disabled, maintaining the interface's consistency between page reloads and prevent accidental data loss. By synchronising the browser's displayed URL with user inputs, users can share their URL or bookmark it to reach the same translation.

In addition to text translation, the toolchain supports web page and document translation. In HTML-Tools, URLs are automatically detected in the source text input and APy handles the fetching and translation of the URL, the result of which is displayed within a `iframe` in HTML-Tools. Any links in the web page are instrumented to also trigger translation. APY's document translation endpoint supports standard text formats including LibreOffice and Microsoft Office.

[14] A technique pioneered by Wynand Winterbach.

[15] `http://www.tornadoweb.org/en/stable/`

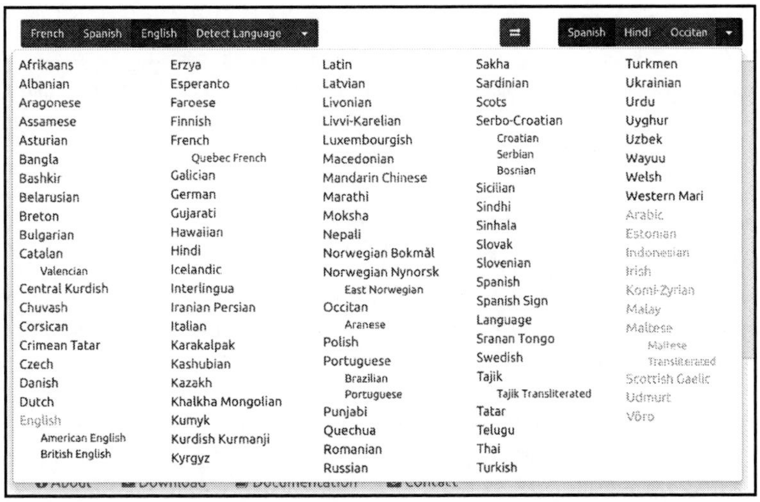

Figure 2: Possible target languages for a translation from English when multi-step translation is enabled (see §5.1) on `beta.apertium.org`.

Aside from the translation mode, HTML-Tools provides other modes visualised as tabs in the interface. Two of these are morphological analysis and generation. The output of morphological analysis has pretty-printing support, and morphological generation of surface forms accepts analyses in Apertium stream format[16]. Another tab is a sandbox mode that facilitates querying APy with arbitrary content, a particularly useful tool for developers. Navigation between modes is synchronised with the browser's URL to ensure consistency for reloads and URL sharing.

HTML-Tools has built-in integration with Matomo (formerly Piwik)[17], a free and open-source web analytics platform, to enable collection of statistics such as which language pairs are most often used (see §6). In a similar vein, APy supports not only the logging of usage statistics, but also the collection of words in translation requests that are unknown to Apertium's translation engine. These words have the potential to serve as seed data for future initiatives aimed at improving language pair performance.

To aid in development, the toolchain is currently configured with linters for JavaScript, HTML, CSS, and Python. These linters and a basic test suite for APy are run via continuous integration platforms CircleCI[18] (HTML-Tools) and Travis CI[19] (APy). A Docker[20] configuration is provided to enable starting the entire toolchain with a single command.

[16] `http://wiki.apertium.org/wiki/Apertium_stream_format`
[17] `https://matomo.org/`
[18] `https://circleci.com/`
[19] `https://travis-ci.org/`
[20] `https://www.docker.com/`

5 Ongoing Work

Several features are in progress and have little work remaining, primarily consisting of merging changes from various contributors into the toolchain and ensuring that the features do not interfere with each other.

5.1 Multi-step Translation

Multi-step translation, i.e. translation with one or more intermediate languages, is supported by APy. An APy request can specify the precise path for translation or can specify just the ultimate source and target languages and allow APy to select an appropriate path.

Currently, multi-step translation involves piping the generated text of one pair into the analyser of another, possibly introducing surface form ambiguity; future work could improve this by bypassing the intermediate generators and analysers and directly passing the morphological analysis between language pairs. Also, when no path is specified, APy chooses a translation path solely by minimising the number of intermediate languages; future work could improve this by introducing some numerical measure of the quality of a pair and hence enabling APy to choose the qualitatively 'best' path.

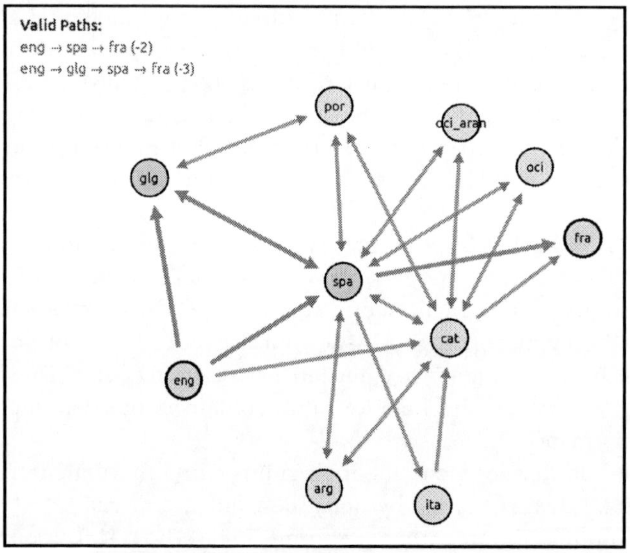

Figure 3: Graphical interface to choose a multi-step translation path from English to French using Apertium's released pairs. Blue nodes are intermediate languages that the user has selected, and green arrows form valid translation paths through those nodes.

A basic interface for multi-step translation has also already been implemented in HTML-Tools[21]. When enabled, multi-step translation allows the user to select any target reachable via a multi-step path from the selected source. However, this approach does not provide any information about or control over the chosen path. To remedy this, an graphical multi-step interface has been developed in HTML-Tools (unreleased). Figure 3 shows a typical interface presented to the user upon selecting English as the source language and French as the ultimate target language. Further, the nodes in the graph are draggable, and information about the selected path is also represented elsewhere in the translation interface.

5.2 Dictionary Lookup

Figure 4 illustrates the dictionary lookup feature of the translation interface. When a translation is requested for a single word, HTML-Tools uses APy's dictionary endpoint to fetch all possible translated lemmas along with their part-of-speech.

Figure 4: Dictionary lookup interface showing possible Spanish translations of the English word 'leaves'.

This functionality has been implemented on feature branches in APy and HTML-Tools, but requires further work prior to release. Specifically, the dictionary mode could provide reverse translations for additional context, grammatical information such as the gender of nouns or the conjugation paradigms of verbs, and information about multi-word lexical units which are currently not handled by HTML-Tools although APy supports dictionary lookup for any lexical unit.

5.3 Spell-Checking

The spell-checking mode of HTML-Tools allows users to spell-check input text in languages that support the feature. The interface is separate from the interfaces for translation, analysis, etc. In APy, spell-checking relies on a speller mode being enabled in a language module; these modes often use libvoikko[22] or hfst-ospell[23].

[21] Enabled, for example, on `turkic.apertium.org`.

[22] `https://github.com/voikko/corevoikko`

[23] `https://github.com/hfst/hfst-ospell`

Generating a mode from an existing language module is fairly simple, requiring only installation of the libraries and tools and small additions to the Makefile.

Implementations of spell-checking on the front and back end are still undergoing testing for robustness and usability, with plans to release them soon.

5.4 Suggestions

The suggestions interface allows users to suggest translations of unknown words, as shown in Figure 5. In APy, support for suggestions is still in development, while the HTML-Tools interface is developed but needs some refinement before release.

(a) An unknown word is highlighted in the output of a Spanish-English translation, and the interface provides an opportunity to offer a suggestion.

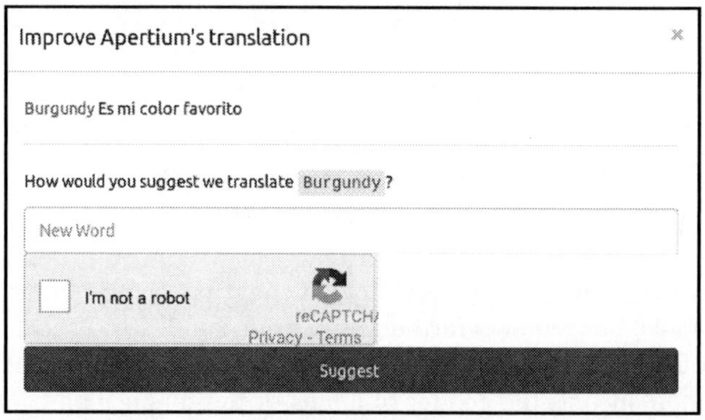

(b) An interface is provided for offering a suggestion. Context is included in the submitted suggestion.

Figure 5: When suggestions are enabled and an unknown word is encountered, users can suggest translations of the word that are sent to an APy endpoint.

Another proposed improvement is providing users the ability to rate translations as 'thumb up/down' or on a numerical scale. This requires less effort for the users and is thus likely to produce more feedback for Apertium, and the numerical ratings could be used as a measure of quality for pairs produced by human evaluation. Such a qualitative measure would be useful for many Apertium applications including multi-step translation path selection (§5.1).

6 Usage Statistics

As discussed in section 4, HTML-Tools supports web analytics via Matomo. In Table 1 we present some statistics from the apertium.org site to testify to the robustness of the toolchain and show trends in end-user behavior and demographics.

Since April 2014, the site has served 2.1 million visits from 183 distinct countries around the world. During this period, the associated APy instance received 19.8 million translation requests. Only ~0.5% of the requests were for document or web page translation, the only other functions exposed on apertium.org.

Table 1 lists the language pairs that have received over one hundred thousand requests. We note that instant translation is enabled by default and typing into the source text input continuously will intermittently trigger translation requests.

Language Pair	Requests (thousands)		Characters (millions)	
nob-nno	12,286	62.3%	7,225	16.8%
spa-cat	2,005	10.2%	7,083	16.5%
nno-nob	726	3.7%	758	1.8%
por-spa	693	3.5%	519	1.2%
spa-cat_valencia	672	3.4%	2,344	5.5%
cat-spa	652	3.3%	9,197	21.4%
eng-spa	544	2.8%	5,376	12.5%
spa-por	318	1.6%	679	1.6%
spa-eng	286	1.5%	1,087	2.5%
eng-cat	151	0.8%	990	2.3%
nob-swe	126	0.6%	62	0.1%

Table 1: Translation requests served by apertium.org grouped by language pairs (using ISO 639-3 codes). Percentages indicate portion of all requests.

7 Conclusion

Perhaps the most important reason why Apertium's web toolchain is well-suited for low-resource languages is that the toolchain enables easy public access to language technology with very low costs and maintenance requirements, allowing developers to spend more funding and time on developing the technology itself. All the software components required to run an online language service are free and open source. Further, their disk, memory, and processing requirements are low enough to work on any personal computer. Once downloaded, even an Internet connection is not required to use these tools.

As mentioned in §2, HTML-Tools provides a free, open source, and customisable interface for custom low-resource language services. The web interface also allows for sub-sites showcasing tools for low-resource languages. An example of such a sub-site is turkic.apertium.org for the Turkic languages in Apertium.

Lastly, features described in §5 have the potential to be greatly beneficial for low-resource languages. Multi-step translation, if used with existing high-quality translation pairs, can produce moderate-quality pairs using intermediate languages with no extra effort, extending the utility and range of possible translations among low-resource languages. The suggestions interface can make it very easy for users of low-resource languages and technology to help their developers improve these tools.

As a free and open-source project, Apertium is driven by its community. We welcome all suggestions, feedback, and pull requests! The HTML-Tools GitHub repository[24] and the APy GitHub repository[25] have their own issue/pull request trackers, while comments about language data or questions about installation are welcome on Apertium's mailing list[26] and Freenode IRC channel, `#apertium` [27].

Beyond technical contributions, we also appreciate help improving HTML-Tools' localisation by revising or extending current ones, or adding new ones.

As current usage by Apertium and other organisations demonstrates, the Apertium web toolchain features a platform that enables end users to quickly benefit from the efforts of mature language technology. A host of improvements in the pipeline from spell-checking to dictionary lookup and a steady stream of contributors signal a promising future.

References

Forcada, M. L. et al. (2011). "Apertium: a free/open-source platform for rule-based machine translation". In: *Machine Translation* 25 (2), pp. 127–144.

Ivars-Ribes, X. and V. M. Sánchez-Cartagena (2011). "A Widely Used Machine Translation Service and its Migration to a Free/Open-Source Solution : the Case of Softcatalà". In: *Proceedings of the Second International Workshop on Free/Open-Source Rule-Based Machine Translation*. URL: http://hdl.handle.net/10609/5648.

Mistry, K. et al. (2017). *Content translation/Machine Translation/Apertium/Service*. URL: https://www.mediawiki.org/wiki/Content_translation/Machine_Translation/Apertium/Service (visited on 2018-02-10).

Sánchez-Cartagena, V. M. and J. A. Pérez-Ortiz (2010). "ScaleMT: a free/open-source framework for building scalable machine translation web services". In: *The Prague Bulletin of Mathematical Linguistics* (93), pp. 97–106.

[24] https://github.com/goavki/apertium-html-tools

[25] https://github.com/goavki/apertium-apy

[26] https://lists.sourceforge.net/lists/listinfo/apertium-stuff

[27] http://wiki.apertium.org/wiki/IRC

Association for Computational Linguistics
209 N. Eighth Street
Stroudsburg, Pennsylvania 18360

ISBN 978-1-5108-6730-7
9 781510 867307

CURRAN ASSOCIATES INC.
proceedings.com